English-Medium Instruction in Turkish Universities

In response to the growing use of English as an international language, the number of English-medium instruction (EMI) programs in higher education has increased. However, decisions to implement EMI programs are often made through top-down policymaking processes with little consideration for the educational issues surrounding language policy changes.

This book examines the variation with which EMI is implemented at universities in Turkey through a multilevel empirical investigation of policies, practices, and perceptions. In addition to providing a sociohistorical overview of EMI in Turkey, the book draws on a dataset that includes policy documents, classroom observations, interviews with teachers, and focus group discussions with students. Despite national policies which envision a "one-language-at-a-time" model of EMI education, this book argues that EMI is neither English-only nor English-always in practice. By highlighting the variation with which EMI is implemented at and across Turkish universities, this study illustrates the need for more comprehensive EMI policies and processes aimed at integrating content and language learning in higher education.

Implications are discussed with respect to policy planning, program development, and pedagogical support and will be relevant for researchers and postgraduate research students interested in EMI, particularly in the Turkish context.

Kari Sahan is Lecturer in Second Language Education at the Institute of Education, University of Reading, Berkshire, England. She is Program Co-director of the MA English Language Education program, delivered in partnership with Guangdong University of Foreign Studies in Guangzhou, China.

Routledge Focus on English-Medium Instruction in Higher Education

The series pulls together experts from around the world who are at the cutting edge of research on EMI within higher education. It presents a balance of research-oriented voices and evidence-based practical guidance for EMI implementation. Contributions will address the phenomenon of EMI from a range of international contexts.

The books in the series focus on contemporary developments in the field, providing concise, up-to-the-minute perspectives and examples to those involved in EMI planning and implementation. This series accepts proposals for books in two formats. The Routledge Focus short-form format is an excellent choice for shorter topics (up to 45,000 words) that reflect the quickly changing EMI research environment. When the topic requires more in-depth analysis, proposals for full-length monographs (up to 100,000 words) will be considered. Please clearly indicate which format you are planning when you submit your proposal.

Researching English-Medium Higher Education
Diverse Applications and Critical Evaluations of the ROAD-MAPPING Framework
Edited by Emma Dafouz and Ute Smit

Input in English-medium Instruction
Edited by Francesca Costa and Cristina Mariotti

EMI Classroom Communication
A Corpus-Based Approach
Edited by Slobodanka Dimova, Joyce Kling and Branka Drljača Margić

English-medium Instruction in Turkish Universities
Policies, Practices, and Perceptions
Kari Sahan

To access the full list of titles, please visit: www.routledge.com/Routledge-Focus-on-English-Medium-Instruction-in-Higher-Education/book-series/RFEHE

English-Medium Instruction in Turkish Universities
Policies, Practices, and Perceptions

Kari Sahan

LONDON AND NEW YORK

First published 2024
by Routledge
4 Park Square, Milton Park, Abingdon, Oxon OX14 4RN

and by Routledge
605 Third Avenue, New York, NY 10158

Routledge is an imprint of the Taylor & Francis Group, an informa business

© 2024 Kari Sahan

The right of Kari Sahan to be identified as author of this work has been asserted in accordance with sections 77 and 78 of the Copyright, Designs and Patents Act 1988.

All rights reserved. No part of this book may be reprinted or reproduced or utilised in any form or by any electronic, mechanical, or other means, now known or hereafter invented, including photocopying and recording, or in any information storage or retrieval system, without permission in writing from the publishers.

Trademark notice: Product or corporate names may be trademarks or registered trademarks, and are used only for identification and explanation without intent to infringe.

British Library Cataloguing-in-Publication Data
A catalogue record for this book is available from the British Library

ISBN: 978-1-032-06531-1 (hbk)
ISBN: 978-1-032-06532-8 (pbk)
ISBN: 978-1-003-20270-7 (ebk)

DOI: 10.4324/9781003202707

Typeset in Times New Roman
by Apex CoVantage, LLC

For Altay

Contents

List of figures viii
List of tables ix
About the author x

1 Introduction 1

2 English-medium instruction in Turkish higher education 8

3 EMI policies in Turkey 18

4 EMI classroom practices 34

5 Teacher and student perceptions 51

6 Conclusion 66

References 76
Index 85

Figures

1.1	Continuum of approaches to language and content teaching	3
3.1	The ROAD-MAPPING framework	20
6.1	EMI language policy arbiters in Turkish higher education	67

Tables

3.1	Medium of instruction offered at HEIs	24
3.2	Language proficiency standards at each HEI	24
3.3	Arrangement of courses in EMI programs	29
4.1	Most common functions of language in EMI classrooms (percentage of class time)	39
4.2	Functions by language according to frequency and percentage of coding	40

About the author

Dr Kari Sahan is Lecturer in Second Language Education at the Institute of Education, University of Reading. She is Program Co-director of the MA English Language Education program, delivered in partnership with Guangdong University of Foreign Studies, in Guangdong, China. Kari is also a member of the EMI Oxford Research group and an Honorary Norham Fellow at the Department of Education, University of Oxford. Prior to completing her PhD, Kari worked as an English instructor in Turkey and for the Turkish Fulbright Commission in Ankara. Kari's research focuses on the use of English as a medium instruction (EMI) and Global Englishes for language teaching. She is especially interested in researching multilingual teaching practices and the use of L1 in EMI classes, as well as student engagement and challenges in EMI, EMI language policy, and EMI teacher pedagogy. Her work has appeared in journals such as *ELT Journal*, *Journal of English for Academic Purposes*, *Language Teaching*, *System*, and *Teaching in Higher Education*.

1 Introduction

With the spread of English as an international language, higher education institutions (HEIs) across the world are increasingly offering academic programs taught through English rather than the local language (Macaro, 2018). English-medium instruction (EMI) has become prevalent at universities in order to prepare local students for the global market and to increase the university's international profile. Although the development of English language skills is usually not an explicit learning outcome of EMI programs, the introduction of EMI brings with it the expectation of dual learning aims. Researchers have noted that a "widely purported benefit of EMI is that it kills two birds with one stone; in other words, [stakeholders assume that] students simultaneously acquire both English and content knowledge" (Rose et al., 2019, p. 2). However, as EMI continues to grow globally, the extent to which these dual aims of content and language learning are achieved remains dubitable, in part due to a lack of clarity regarding the relationship between EMI policy and practice.

In their conceptual piece striving for a definition of EMI with "comparative equivalence," Rose et al. (2021) emphasize that there is no "one-size-fits-all" approach to EMI. Instead, countries have taken different approaches to EMI implementation. In some contexts, EMI programs are not regulated by formal national policies (e.g., Italy, Spain), while in other contexts, the expansion of EMI has been led by government initiatives (e.g., China, Japan). In still other contexts, governmental support for EMI has oscillated over the years (e.g., Malaysia, United Arab Emirates). Commenting on the diversity with which EMI is carried out within and across countries, Dearden and Macaro (2016) state that

> [T]here is an urgent need for research to establish whether this diversity is a positive reflection of different cultural needs, or whether it is simply an overall lack of understanding of EMI's implications and of poor investment in programme preparation.
>
> (p. 476)

DOI: 10.4324/9781003202707-1

Guided by this call for research, this book explores the implementation of EMI policies and practices in higher education in Turkey. It does so by drawing on the empirical findings of a large-scale study, investigating EMI across seven state universities. Before exploring the implementation of EMI at Turkish universities, this introductory chapter will define EMI and contextualize its global growth.

1.1 Defining English-medium instruction

In this book, EMI is defined as: "The use of the English language to teach academic subjects (other than English itself) in countries or jurisdictions where the first language (L1) of the majority of the population is not English" (Macaro, 2018, p. 19). According to this definition, language learning is not an explicit aim or outcome of EMI, since English is used to teach academic content but is not the academic content itself.

As such, EMI is conceptually distinct from other forms of second language (L2) education, including English language teaching (ELT), content-based instruction (CBI), immersion education, and content and language integrated learning (CLIL) in which the instruction is, to varying degrees, explicitly focused on L2 learning (Macaro, 2018; Pecorari & Malmström, 2018). In ELT, or English as a foreign language (EFL) classes, English is taught as the subject material. The goal in ELT/EFL classes is to improve students' L2 skills. CBI is an approach to language teaching which integrates nonlinguistic content to enhance language instruction. By some definitions, CBI is conceptually similar to CLIL, which is defined as a "dual-focused form of instruction where attention is given to both the language and the content" (Coyle et al., 2010, p. 3). Lasagabaster and Sierra (2010) note that CLIL programs are distinct from language immersion programs in that the target language in CLIL is a language which is not spoken locally, whereas immersion programs are often taught in a local or minority language to which students would have exposure outside of class, either at home or in society. Although definitions of CLIL do not specify English as the target language, the majority of CLIL programs in Europe are conducted in English (Lasagabaster & Sierra, 2010).

Galloway and Rose (2021) describe a continuum along which approaches to language and content teaching can be categorized and compared according to the degree of emphasis placed on content and language learning (Figure 1.1). EFL classes are positioned on the "language-dominant" end of the spectrum, while EMI classes are positioned on the opposite side, the "content-dominant" end. CLIL and CBI are placed along the middle of the spectrum, since language and content learning are both explicit aims, with the emphasis on each varying according to context. According to this conceptual understanding of EMI, any language learning benefits resulting from EMI are incidental and due to exposure to English during content teaching, rather than explicit language instruction in class.

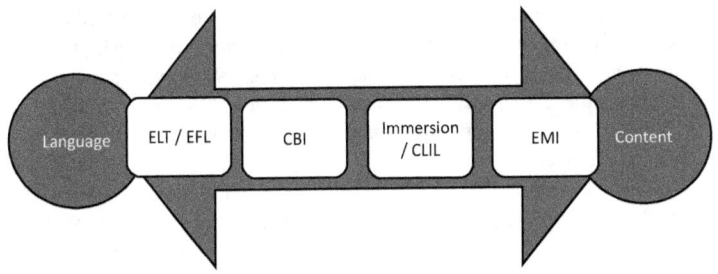

Figure 1.1 Continuum of approaches to language and content teaching (adapted from Galloway & Rose, 2020)

Despite this conceptual definition of EMI, EMI programs are often framed by policymakers, practitioners, and other stakeholders as an opportunity for students to improve their English language skills (Moncada-Comas & Block, 2019; Shohamy, 2013). This line of thinking posits that a motivation for introducing EMI is that it will "expose students to large quantities of the target language" (Macaro, Tian, et al., 2018, p. 1) as they learn through an English immersion environment. However, Moncada-Comas and Block (2019) have argued that EMI becomes "CLIL-ized" when it is adopted for the purpose of improving students' English proficiency. Although stakeholders may envision a "CLIL-ized" version of EMI, Moncada-Comas and Block (2019) argue that this assumption of language learning "is based on a naïve theory of second language acquisition, according to which language learning takes place by osmosis, simply via exposure to content in English due to EMI's immersive nature" (p. 687). Indeed, empirical evidence has cast doubt on the effectiveness of EMI for language learning (see Macaro, Curle, et al., 2018) and has repeatedly demonstrated that content lecturers do not incorporate language teaching into their classes (Airey, 2012; Block & Moncada-Comas, 2019). These teaching practices are distinct from CLIL in which the language is integrated into teaching and learning activities. In other words, although language learning might be an implicit or assumed outcome of EMI, empirical evidence has suggested that is not necessarily realized in practice.

1.2 Understanding the growth of EMI

In recent years, EMI has grown rapidly at the university level. Some of the most comprehensive studies concerning the expansion of EMI have emerged from Europe. Two of these studies (Brenn-White & Faethe, 2013; Wächter & Maiworm, 2015) included large-scale surveys on the number of EMI programs offered by country. These surveys have found that the number of EMI programs offered at European universities has increased exponentially over the past decade, especially in northern and western Europe. The Netherlands and Germany have been reported to offer the largest number of EMI programs while Denmark and Sweden have shown the highest growth rates (Brenn-White & Faethe, 2013). Across European countries, these surveys have also found that the most common disciplines for EMI study are business and economics or engineering and technology.

The expansion of EMI in Europe has been traced to the Bologna Process (Smit & Dafouz, 2012; Unterberger, 2012), which was started in 1999 and has created networks of cooperation between European universities. The Bologna Process consists of intergovernmental agreements signed by European countries to establish the European Higher Education Area, which has facilitated staff and student mobility through programs such as Erasmus. As a result of increased collaboration and mobility between universities in Europe, English is used as a lingua franca (ELF) for communication, teaching, and research. Kerklaan et al. (2008) have suggested that EMI programs facilitate the mobility of staff and students by removing language barriers to education. On average, 54% of students in EMI programs in Europe in 2014 were international students (Wächter & Maiworm, 2015). The nature of EMI programs in Europe, therefore, appears to be largely international in focus or at least inter-European.

Given this backdrop, the research on EMI in Europe has focused on multilingual practices in EMI university contexts (Dafouz & Smit, 2016; Kuteeva, 2020), EMI teachers' identities and beliefs (Airey, 2012; Moncada-Comas & Block, 2019), and the effectiveness of EMI teacher training programs (Dafouz, 2018; Sánchez-Pérez, 2020). Much of this research has focused on embracing multilingualism within the context of inter-European exchange, with Dafouz and Smit (2020) proposing the term "English-Medium Education in Multilingual University Settings" (EMEMUS) in place of EMI.

Outside of Europe, the growth of EMI at the university level has been documented in contexts such as Japan (Aizawa & Rose, 2019; Bradford & Brown, 2017), China (Hu & Lei, 2014; Jiang et al., 2019), Hong Kong (Evans & Morrison, 2011; Pun & Macaro, 2019), and the Middle East (Graham et al., 2021; Hopkyns & Gkonou, 2023). Existing research on EMI in these contexts has focused on policy implementation (Rose & McKinley, 2018; Ali, 2013) and the effectiveness of EMI for content and language learning (Rose et al., 2019; Hu & Lei, 2014). Research from across Asia and the Middle East has also contributed critical global perspectives on EMI, challenging its Western-centric positioning (Rose et al., 2022).

Similarly, research on EMI from the Global South has highlighted some of the inequalities associated with EMI education. Although comparatively less research on EMI has been conducted in these contexts (see Sahan et al., 2021), much of this research has offered critical perspectives of EMI which are largely absent from research in Europe. For example, Sah (2022) has argued that EMI policies at the schooling level in Nepal perpetuate inequalities for marginalized groups. EMI is positioned as a privileged form of linguistic

Introduction 5

capital in Nepal, underpinned by assumptions that studying through English leads upward mobility, despite the reality of negative outcomes for many marginalized children (Sah & Li, 2018). Similarly, in India, Annamalai (2013) has argued that there is a "hidden social cost of the spread of English-medium education" (p. 192), whereby EMI is associated with the promise of economic success—a myth that Annamalai refers to as "the falsity of English" that is rarely realized by students who lack access to high-quality education.

Still, few studies at the tertiary level have investigated national EMI policies and their translation to classroom practices. Driven by top-down economic considerations rather than educational motivations (Piller & Cho, 2013), EMI policy often disadvantages students with low English proficiency and "exacerbates socioeconomic inequalities in the country" (Selvi, 2014, p. 143). To this end, Turkey offers a unique case study as a country of unequal socioeconomic development and a border country with Europe, partially but unevenly integrated into the European higher education system. Understanding EMI in Turkey is important, because "English is increasingly going to become a 'commodity' of those belonging to the upper middle class" (Selvi, 2011, p. 196). As such, this book contributes to our understanding of teachers' and students' experiences with EMI policy and practice.

1.3 EMI and internationalization

As noted at the beginning of this chapter, the internationalization of HE is often cited as a motivation for the introduction or expansion of EMI programs. EMI is perceived as a means through which HEIs can recruit international staff, attract international students (who often pay higher tuition fees), increase university rankings, and prepare domestic students for the international job market (Brenn-White & Faethe, 2013; Wächter & Maiworm, 2015). English is often considered a desirable language of education because strong English skills are equated with better job prospects and higher salaries (Piller & Cho, 2013; Şahan & Sahan, 2023).

As De Costa et al. (2019) have argued, "English is often valorized as the global language par excellence that facilitates global business and economic development" (p. 396). This "valorization" of English has led some scholars to suggest that "English" and "international" have become conflated in the discourse of higher education, whereby internationalization has become synonymous with "Englishization" (Kirkpatrick, 2011; Phillipson, 2008). Similarly, Coleman (2006) has suggested that the spread of EMI has adverse effects on local languages, and other scholars have highlighted the extent to which fears of domain loss propel opposition to EMI policy (Hultgren, 2013).

Thus, the introduction of EMI for the purposes of internationalization alters the language landscape at the university (Doiz et al., 2013). Piller and Cho (2013) are critical of what they consider the "illusion of a meritocracy" (p. 39) in English education and instead characterize English as a gatekeeper to quality education. This notion extends to the assumptions of EMI being associated with "better" or more elite programs at HEIs globally. In response to the dominant role of English in higher education, some scholars have suggested that language education policy should incorporate support for multilingual learners (Shohamy, 2013). In line with these calls, this books explores EMI implementation in Turkish higher education by examining language policy and (multilingual) language practices.

1.4 Overview of the book

A recent systematic review of EMI in higher education concluded that in Turkey, "the collective research picture is one of deep concern in terms of level of English in general and vocabulary knowledge in particular" (Macaro, Curle, et al., 2018, p. 53). Given these "deep concerns" regarding English proficiency, as well as considerations for the role of English in the internationalization of HE, this book focuses its attention on the role of English in EMI policy and practice in Turkey.

Previous research on EMI has examined stakeholders' beliefs through survey data (Costa & Coleman, 2012; Macaro & Akincioglu, 2018), analyzed top-down EMI policymaking process, (Ali, 2013; Rose & McKinley, 2018), and investigated classroom language use through single case studies (Duran & Sert, 2019; Tarnopolsky & Goodman, 2014). What is missing from this body of research is an examination of how, or to what extent, policy provisions are interpreted and implemented by the teachers and students engaged in EMI education across a diversity of classrooms in a national context. As such, this book addresses that gap by exploring the policies, practices, and perceptions that characterize undergraduate EMI engineering programs at state universities in Turkey. The data for the study reported in this book were collected from a large-scale study (Sahan, 2020) which examined EMI implementation at the macro-level (national), meso-level (institutional), and micro-level (classroom) through the analysis of policy documents, classroom observations, and in-depth interviews with teachers and students. The seven universities included in this study were selected to represent an array of EMI contexts in order to provide empirical evidence to support better theory, policies, and language support structures for EMI teachers and students. To this end, the book is guided by the following overarching research question:

> *With what variation is EMI implemented in undergraduate engineering programs in Turkey?*

In addressing its overarching research question, the following sub-questions are answered in Chapters 3, 4, and 5, respectively:

- Chapter 3: *What are the current national and institutional policies for EMI engineering programs in Turkey, and how do these EMI policies vary across universities?*

- Chapter 4: *How are languages used in university-level EMI engineering classes in Turkey?*
- Chapter 5: *How do teachers and students perceive EMI in university-level engineering programs in Turkey?*

Chapter 2 provides an overview of EMI in Turkish higher education and explores the research literature on EMI in Turkey. It traces the development of EMI in Turkish higher education and highlights key challenges and opportunities for EMI at Turkish universities.

Then, Chapter 3 presents the results of the policy analysis using the ROAD-MAPPING framework (Dafouz & Smit, 2016). This chapter describes national and institutional policies regulating EMI at universities in Turkey. The ROAD-MAPPING framework is applied to analyze 145 policy documents. The analysis presented in this chapter explores how national-level policies were appropriated and reflected at the institutional level. Different institutions are compared to reveal the diversity and similarity of EMI policies at Turkish universities.

Chapter 4 presents the results from the analysis of classroom observation data to explore EMI language practices. This chapter draws on classroom observation data from 21 EMI teachers at seven universities. Each teacher's class was observed twice, for a total of 85 classroom observations, which were analyzed using a structured coding scheme. The findings from the classroom observations presented in this chapter show how English and Turkish are used for teaching and learning in EMI classrooms.

Next, Chapter 5 presents findings on teachers' and students' perceptions of EMI policy and practice. This chapter presents data from semi-structured interviews with teachers and focus group discussions with students. In total, 21 teachers (who participated in classroom observations for Chapter 4) were interviewed, and 25 focus groups discussions were conducted with their students. The findings presented in this chapter shed light on teachers' and students' perceptions of teaching and learning in EMI contexts.

Chapters 3, 4, and 5 contextualize the diversity of EMI policies and practices found across EMI engineering classrooms in Turkey. Finally, Chapter 6 synthesizes the findings from the previous chapters and offers conclusions for researchers and practitioners.

In examining the variation with which EMI policies are implemented and the practices that characterize language use across classroom settings, this book makes empirical and theoretical contributions to research on EMI, and its contents are of value to researchers, teachers, and policymakers who are interested in improving the quality of EMI education.

2 English-medium instruction in Turkish higher education

Given Turkey's history, diversity, and geopolitical positioning, it is a compelling context for the examination of English-medium instruction (EMI) policies and practices. Turkey has been characterized as a bridge between East and West, possessing traits of both Europe and the Middle East but uniquely distinct from both regions. Although it was never colonized, Selvi (2011) claims that Turkey shares sociolinguistic characteristics with some post-colonial societies because of its sociopolitical history and the importance of English. Many of Turkey's universities are members of the Bologna Process and participate in student and staff mobility exchange programs with European universities. However, the enactment of and participation in these programs vary across institutions. Given Turkey's unique position, it is important to study the Turkish case in order to understand how EMI practices differ across classrooms and what the implications of this variation are for EMI education in practice.

This chapter provides an overview of EMI in Turkish higher education. It begins by tracing the history of EMI in Turkey, noting the origins of foreign language medium of instruction (MoI) during Ottoman times. It traces this history to the current state of EMI in Turkish higher education, and it explores key findings from research on Turkey with respect to English language proficiency and challenges; learning outcomes and academic success in EMI programs; and classroom practices, including the use of translanguaging in EMI. This chapter provides the contextual background on EMI in Turkey, setting the stage for the empirical research findings presented in Chapters 3, 4, and 5 of this book.

2.1 History of EMI in the Turkey

In Turkey, where English is connected with concepts of modernization and Westernization, EMI has historically been connected with elite education (Selvi, 2014). Although the growth of EMI is a relatively recent phenomenon, the history of EMI in Turkey dates back to Ottoman times with the founding of Robert College in 1863 by American missionaries. During this period,

DOI: 10.4324/9781003202707-2

English-medium instruction in Turkish higher education 9

secondary schools founded by foreign (American or European) missionary groups typically provided education in the language of these groups. Kırkgöz (2007) has suggested that the introduction of these secondary schools was connected with efforts to Westernize the education system during the Ottoman Tanzimat period of reform in the mid-19th century (Kırkgöz, 2007). In addition to Robert College, Galatasaray Lisesi was founded by French missionaries in 1868, and Üsküdar American College by American missionaries in 1876. These schools remain operational today as three of the most elite secondary schools in the country, and they continue to provide instruction in English or French.

At the secondary school level, Anatolian high schools (*Anadolu liseleri*) were established in 1955 as public high schools to provide intensive foreign language instruction through EMI. The curriculum at Anatolian high schools included a one-year intensive English language preparatory program, known as *hazırlık*. Students completed the one-year *hazırlık* program before beginning their EMI courses (Kırkgöz, 2007). However, this system of EMI at Anatolian high schools was abolished in 2006, with the intensive English language preparatory year abandoned in 2005 (Selvi, 2014; Kırkgöz, 2007). Anatolian high schools have since offered Turkish-medium instruction (TMI) for content area courses and EFL classes for foreign language education. Today, EMI at the secondary level is largely limited to elite private schools and a small handful of selective public high schools.

At the level of higher education, EMI was first introduced with the establishment of Middle East Technical University (METU) in 1956, a public university in Ankara. Historically connected to Robert College, Boğaziçi University became the second public university to offer EMI education in 1971, when it was converted into a public HEI. Two of the most elite universities in the country, METU and Boğaziçi, teach entirely through EMI and were the only public EMI universities until the expansion of the university system in the early 2000s. More commonly, EMI programs were offered by private universities, beginning with the founding of Bilkent University in Ankara in 1984 (Selvi, 2014; Kırkgöz, 2007). Because access to EMI education has historically been limited to the upper class through these elite and often private institutions, researchers have asserted that EMI "exacerbates socioeconomic inequalities in the country" (Selvi, 2014, p. 143).

Throughout the last two decades, the number of public universities in Turkey has increased dramatically through a government-led initiative to expand higher education starting in 2008. In 2005, there were 73 HEIs in Turkey; by 2010, the number of HEIs had increased to 156 (Günay & Günay, 2011). In 2019, there were 207 HEIs in Turkey, of which 129 were state universities (YÖK, 2019). Despite their young histories, many of these newly established universities offer EMI programs. Recent estimates suggest that approximately 50% of state universities and 70% of private universities in Turkey offer at least one undergraduate program taught through English (Kırkgöz et al.,

2023). The expansion of EMI in higher education, particularly in the public sector, has broadened the scope, range, and profile of students and teachers engaged in EMI higher education in Turkey. With this expansion of EMI programs in Turkey, researchers have charted what Selvi (2014) refers to as "oscillating" debates. These debates are governed by a tension between perceptions that, on the one hand, English is an important language for achieving instrumental aims, such as economic gain and career advancement (Kırkgöz, 2007, 2009; Uçar & Soruç, 2018), and, on the other hand, that EMI is a threat to Turkish language and culture (Sinanoğlu, 2004; Büyükkantarcıoğlu, 2004). Concerns about "the degeneration and alienation of the Turkish language" due to the incursion of EMI have been expressed by scholars, politicians, and laypeople alike (Aslan, 2018, p. 609). From the perspective of top-down policymaking, preliminary findings from a large-scale study into the growth of EMI across Europe have suggested that university policymakers and industry stakeholders in Turkey oppose the use of EMI (Yuksel et al., 2023c). Research has also found opposition from a bottom-up perspective: in a recent study, Selvi (2022) demonstrates how grassroots' opposition to EMI is constructed through social media posts drawing on national images, quotes, and actors. Many opponents of EMI argue that it prevents the development of Turkish terminology in the fields of science and technology where there are no Turkish equivalents for English loans words (Büyükkantarcıoğlu, 2004). Combined with the increasing presence of English in media, such arguments are extended to suggest that the increasing number of English loan words in everyday life jeopardizes the purity of the Turkish language (Selvi, 2011) and threatens local cultural identity. Indeed, some previous empirical research has found that students enrolled in university EMI programs felt distant from their L1 culture (Kırkgöz, 2009) and were concerned about not being able to express field-related terminology in Turkish (Dearden & Akincioglu, 2016).

Nonetheless, despite this opposition, EMI in higher education has been promoted in connection with scientific research and framed as a benefit to HEIs through increased international exchange opportunities and access to scientific publications in English (Alptekin & Tatar, 2011; Kırkgöz, 2007). Aside from its role as an academic lingua franca, English serves instrumental purposes for career advancement in Turkey, such as through financial bonuses offered at work based on English examination scores (*yabancı dil tazmınatı*). Scores from English proficiency exams are considered for hiring purposes, particularly scores on the national standardized language assessment (*Yabancı Dil Sınavı*, YDS). Indeed, research has consistently demonstrated that the motivation to study EMI courses is tied to the belief that EMI will contribute to students' language development and positive career advancement (Şahan & Sahan, 2023; Sahan & Şahan, 2021; Altay & Yuksel, 2021).

These ongoing debates highlight the complex role of EMI in Turkish society. In addition to the sociolinguistic and cultural implications of EMI, researchers have examined EMI from an educational perspective, focusing on issues of language proficiency, learning outcomes, and classroom practices. The following sections explore these themes in detail.

2.2 Language proficiency and challenges in EMI programs

The majority of teachers and students engaged in EMI programs globally use English as a second or additional language (L2). Thus, concerns about language proficiency and language-related challenges arising from the use of L2 English are common in EMI research (see Macaro, Curle, et al., 2018). Turkey is no exception to this trend. In fact, a recent systematic review conducted by Macaro, Curle, et al. (2018, p. 52) concluded: "In Turkey, the collective research picture is one of deep concern in terms of level of English in general and vocabulary knowledge in particular."

These language challenges persist despite the provision of the English preparatory program (EPP, or *hazırlık*) in Turkey, which research has found to be insufficient for preparing students for EMI courses (Ekoç, 2020; Kırkgöz, 2009). Challenges identified with the EPP include an inadequate curriculum for teaching academic English, insufficient resources, and low student motivation, in part due to role of the EPP as a bridge between secondary school and university departmental classes. Due to this "in-between" position of the preparatory program, research has suggested that preparatory year students may be less engaged in their English language learning since they do not feel a strong sense of belonging as "real university students" (Kemaloglu-Er, 2023).

Given this background, previous research on EMI in Turkey has examined the language challenges faced by students in EMI settings (Kamaşak et al., 2021; Soruç et al., 2021) and the strategies used to overcome these challenges (Soruç & Griffiths, 2018; Soruç et al., 2018). Studies have suggested that because of language-related challenges, EMI students in Turkey achieve lower academic attainment (Sert, 2008) and have difficulty taking notes (Zok, 2010), asking questions in class (Dalkız, 2002), and understanding technical vocabulary (Yıldız et al., 2017). Moreover, research has repeatedly found that EMI teachers in Turkey perceive their students' English proficiency to be inadequate for EMI study (Başıbek et al., 2014) and that students report challenges understanding content taught through English (Bozdoğan & Karlıdağ, 2013; Kırkgöz, 2014). These findings of ongoing language challenges are matched by studies which have suggested that teachers and students use Turkish in EMI programs to compensate for poor English skills (Kılıçkaya, 2006), a theme which will be explored in more detail in Section 2.4.

In a recent study, Kamaşak et al. (2021) examined the linguistic challenges that EMI students faced at a private university in Istanbul. The study used a validated questionnaire, which was originally developed by Evans and Morrison (2011) in Hong Kong, to explore the areas of academic English with which students had the most difficulty and to examine whether certain groups of students experienced greater linguistic challenges than others. Their findings showed that students faced the most difficulties with the productive skills of writing and speaking in their EMI classes. Specifically, students reported that "using appropriate academic style" was the most challenging aspect of writing, and "participating actively in discussion" was the most challenging aspect of speaking. With respect to individual differences, male students found listening to lectures in English more difficult than female students; students studying in social science subjects found writing and reading more difficult than their peers in engineering disciplines; and local Turkish students found EMI to be more linguistically challenging overall than international students enrolled at the same university. These findings offer implications for English language support classes in Turkey—namely, that students would benefit from more support in developing their academic writing skills and using academic English to participate in class discussions.

In a study looking at the factors which predict the severity of EMI students' language challenges, self-efficacy and motivation were found to have the greatest predictive power in determining students' ease of EMI learning (Sahan et al., 2023). In other words, students with more self-efficacy and motivation experienced fewer language challenges, suggesting the importance of building EMI students' self-beliefs. Student motivation may be particularly important in the Turksih context, where research has found mixed results regarding students' motivation to study through EMI. Some studies have found relatively high levels of motivation among EMI students (Macaro & Akincioglu, 2018; Turhan & Kırkgöz, 2018; Uçar & Soruç, 2018). However, the findings from these studies have also suggested that the motivation to study through EMI decreases as students advance in their undergraduate degree programs; in other words, these studies have found that students further along in their courses were less convinced of the benefits of EMI than first-year students (Macaro & Akincioglu, 2018; Turhan & Kırkgöz, 2018).

Macaro and Akincioglu (2018) investigated the motivations and beliefs of students enrolled in EMI university programs through an online questionnaire; the results of the study were also reported in Dearden and Akincioglu (2016). The study, which included students from 18 universities, found that only 59% of EMI students believed that studying in English was beneficial (Dearden & Akincioglu, 2016). The findings also revealed that private university students were more positive about the benefits of EMI and their experiences studying through EMI than students enrolled to state universities (Macaro & Akincioglu, 2018). However, 60% of the respondents were enrolled in English preparatory programs, meaning that the study is limited in that a majority of respondents had not yet taken an EMI class.

Other studies have also suggested that Turkish university students in EMI programs lack motivation to learn English, despite receiving English support through the EPP (Sert, 2008). Low or decreasing levels of student motivation raise questions about the purpose of EMI in Turkey, particularly if EMI students are not convinced of its benefits. The question of how best to motivate students and support them with their English language learning is an important one, since research has found that English language proficiency may predict academic success (Soruc et al., 2021; Kamaşak & Sahan, 2023). The following sections explore research on academic success in EMI in more detail.

2.3 Learning outcomes in EMI programs

Early research from the Turkish context suggested that EMI resulted in reduced understanding of academic content (Kırkgöz, 2014; Sert, 2008). These early studies on EMI learning outcomes in Turkey primarily explored the concept of academic success through students' perceptions. In other words, they evaluated whether students perceived a loss to content learning through EMI compared to Turkish-medium instruction (TMI). For example, Kırkgöz (2014) compared fourth-year EMI and TMI engineering students' perceptions of the benefits and challenges of content and language learning in their courses using a partially open-ended questionnaire and focus group interviews. The results of the study indicated that MoI was perceived to affect content learning, and the study found that EMI presented (or was perceived to present) obstacles for both language acquisition and content comprehension.

More recent research into learning outcomes on EMI programs in Turkey has taken a quantitative approach to measure the extent to which different factors contribute to students' learning outcomes in EMI. A series of studies conducted by researchers at the University of Bath (UK) and Kocaeli University (Turkey) have sought to quantitatively examine the factors which contribute to or impede students' academic success in EMI programs. The findings from these four studies are summarized here:

(1) Curle et al. (2020) found that general English proficiency, as measured according to students' scores from an in-house proficiency exam, was not a statistically significant predictor of students' academic success in EMI, as measured by their final course scores. However, students' academic success in their TMI classes did predict their success in EMI classes. Based on these findings, the authors have suggested that a multilingual model of EMI, in which L1 use is encouraged, may be more appropriate than a monolingual approach to support students' learning. However, one limitation of the study is that it did not incorporate classroom observations or a measure of language use in the EMI classes, meaning that it is unclear to what extent the students' L1 was (already) used in their EMI classes.

(2) In a follow-up study that compared academic success by discipline, the research team found that English language proficiency was a predictor of academic success for students studying in the social sciences but not for students in the mathematical, physical, and life sciences (Altay et al., 2022). For students studying mathematical, physical, and life sciences,

their success in TMI classes predicted their success in EMI classes—mirroring the findings from Curle et al. (2020). Thus, academic discipline may affect the relationship between English language proficiency and content learning in EMI.

(3) In a longitudinal study looking at the students' language learning gains, the same research group found that EMI students' English language proficiency improved over a period of four years (i.e., throughout their undergraduate program) and that improvements in English language proficiency predicted academic achievement in EMI classes (Yuksel et al., 2023a). In this study, English language proficiency was measured according to an in-house exam adapted from the Cambridge Preliminary English Test (PET).

(4) Similar results in terms of an increase in language proficiency after four years of EMI study were reported in their final study (Soruc et al., 2021). This study also found that students' English language proficiency predicted their language-related challenges in EMI courses and that the minimum threshold of English language proficiency required for EMI study appeared to vary by discipline.

The findings from Yuksel et al. (2023a) and Soruc et al. (2021) support the notion that EMI contributes positively to students' English language development, although the authors do not quantify the gains or describe what this improvement might mean in terms of language proficiency—for example, with respect to the Common European Framework of Reference (CEFR), thus leaving unresolved the question of whether EMI is more effective at improving student proficiency over a four-year period compared to TMI courses plus additional EFL classes. Moreover, because these findings on learning through EMI came from the same project, it is difficult to determine how they might be replicated in other contexts.

Other research in Turkey has examined the relationship among students' EMI academic success and their language learning mindsets (Yuksel et al., 2021), their self-regulation skills (Yuksel et al., 2023b), and their language-related challenges (Kamaşak & Sahan, 2023). Collectively, these studies have contributed to our understanding of the factors that influence successful language and content learning through EMI at Turkish universities. They offer some positive evidence of language learning gains, although questions still remain as to which teaching practices best support successful student learning through EMI, as none of these studies incorporated classroom observations. EMI classroom practices are explored in the next section.

2.4 Classroom practices in EMI programs

So far, this chapter has considered challenges experienced in EMI programs due to limitations with students' English language proficiency as well as potential challenges to students' content learning outcomes as a result of studying through EMI. What is missing from this research is an understanding of *how* EMI is delivered in classrooms. In other words, what are the classroom practices that characterize EMI programs in Turkey?

Research looking at classroom practices in Turkey has generally taken two approaches: (1) it has explored the reported practices of teachers and students, including their beliefs about practices which contribute to successful learning, and (2) it has examined teaching practices through classroom observations. These two approaches to research on classroom practices are discussed next.

In an early study which considered teachers' reported practices, Sert (2008) found that university lecturers preferred TMI over EMI because they believed that TMI more effectively supported content learning. Other early studies investigating the perceptions of EMI teachers reported similar findings: these studies showed that, although EMI teachers reported some advantages to teaching through English (e.g., access to English resources), they preferred teaching in Turkish because it allowed them "to go deeper into the content of the lesson" (Basıbek et al., 2014, p. 1822; see also Kılıçkaya, 2006). This preference for Turkish was reported as being primarily due to language challenges which prevented students from understanding content taught in English. In other words, teachers reported that the L1 was a useful resource, at least in classes where all students were local Turkish students. Karakas (2016) found that while many EMI teachers looked favorably upon L1 use in class, they opposed the use of Turkish when international students were present, so as not to exclude international students linguistically. However, these early studies were largely based on teachers' and students' self-reported practices. Thus, it is difficult to determine the extent to which these teachers' views on language use are borne out in their EMI teaching practices.

In recent years, research on EMI classroom practices in Turkey has incorporated data from classroom observations to examine what teachers and students do in the classrooms. Many of these studies have taken a Conversation Analysis approach to investigate the multimodal resources used by teachers and students in preference organization (Duran & Sert, 2019) and word search sequences (Duran et al., 2022), and conveying disciplinary knowledge (Bozbiyik & Morton, 2023). These studies have contributed to our understanding of how teachers and students in Turkey negotiate meaning in English. Other studies have focused on the strategies used by EMI lecturers (Ege et al., 2022) and students (Soruç & Griffiths, 2018) to teach through English. Still other research has examined patterns of classroom interaction. For example, Genc and Yuksel (2021) investigated EMI teachers' questioning practices through a qualitative study which examined 19 hours of video-recorded lectures. Their findings revealed that the questioning practices of EMI teachers in Turkey did not lead to rich classroom interaction. Instead, teachers tended to use text-based, display questions to check students' learning. Because these questions tended to be closed-ended with an expected or correct answer, Genc and Yuksel (2021) argue that these patterns of questioning limited the length of students' responses. These findings in the Turkish context match those of other contexts (e.g., Pun & Macaro, 2019, in Hong Kong), which have found that EMI teachers tend to ask low-order questions in English, leading to limited opportunities for extended teacher-student interaction.

Other recent research on EMI classroom practices in Turkey has examined language use through the lens of translanguaging (Ataş, 2023; Inci-Kavak & Kırkgöz, 2022; Kırkgöz et al., 2023). While early studies on L1 use in EMI framed Turkish use as the result of low student or teacher proficiency (as noted earlier), research on translanguaging has moved away from a deficit perspective of L1 use in the classroom to a more inclusive paradigm which recognizes the multilingual resources of multilingual learners (see Sahan & Rose, 2021). This recent research has chosen to explore "how translanguaging practices respond to different learning and interaction needs" in Turkish EMI classrooms (Kırkgöz et al., 2023, p. 1). It has found that translanguaging is a common feature of EMI and that both EMI students and teachers tend to hold positive attitudes toward translanguaging practices (Karakaş, 2023; Kırkgöz & Küçük, 2021).

However, many of these studies have come from "soft EMI" subjects such as English literature or from single case studies of EMI classrooms. Less is known about EMI classroom practices across institutions and in "hard EMI" subjects (i.e., disciplines not related to language or linguistics). Given this growing body of research, more evidence is needed to understand how these classroom practices vary across EMI contexts in Turkey and how they contribute to students' learning.

2.5 Conclusion

This chapter has examined the historical development of EMI at Turkish universities from the perspective of policy and perceptions. It has noted that, although EMI is not a new phenomenon in Turkey, it is the subject of ongoing public debate. Supporters of EMI point to the professional and educational benefits of learning (through) English, while opponents of EMI argue that it is a threat to Turkish language, culture, and knowledge development. Research has demonstrated the complexity of EMI in Turkey: while language proficiency seems to be an important factor which contributes to the successful implementation of EMI—and while low English proficiency is frequently cited as an obstacle to EMI—English proficiency alone does not seem determine successful EMI implementation in Turkey.

Nonetheless, EMI research has repeatedly suggested that teachers and students do experience language-related challenges, despite the EPP. It is assumed that students who meet the English proficiency standards of the EPP have the necessary language competences to engage effectively in their EMI lessons. However, given concerns about language proficiency raised in the research findings discussed in this chapter, the question remains as to how effective these policies are in providing for the equal implementation of EMI programs across classroom contexts.

Much of the research concerning EMI education in Turkey has been conducted at single case study institutions, with many of these studies coming from private or elite universities and major urban centers. These universities may have access to a wide range of resources, including the ability to recruit international staff and students, which are not necessarily available to all HEIs. As such, these research contexts do not reflect the diversity of EMI programs in Turkey. Despite centralized policies in Turkey, Kırkgöz (2007) has argued that "due to relative heterogeneous conditions and variations in the facilities and socioeconomic condition in certain regions, it is expected that each school might have context-specific problems" (p. 189). Research is thus needed to examine the policies and practices shaping EMI across HEI contexts.

Further, many empirical studies examining EMI in the Turkish context have relied on questionnaires and interview data to assess (perceptions of) educational practices. Less research has involved classroom observations to provide in-depth analysis of the language used by students and teachers, although there is growing research interest in this area, particularly with respect to understanding translanguaging practices. Still, the expansion of EMI university programs in Turkey requires further classroom-based research.

In other words, what remains to be seen is what practices and policies characterize EMI across Turkish universities, and whether these practices and policies vary between universities. With this in mind, this book now sets out to examine the language practices that shape EMI in Turkey, highlighting how EMI is implemented across HEI contexts. The following chapters seek to address these questions by presenting the findings from three sub-studies, derived from a large-scale study, to investigate EMI implementation at Turkish universities.

3 EMI policies in Turkey

This chapter explores national and institution English-medium instruction (EMI) policies in Turkey. Within the field of applied linguistics, language policy and planning (LPP) is understood to involve the complex interaction of multiple linguistic and nonlinguistic variables (Spolsky, 2004). Language policies often reproduce standard language ideologies, including notions of correctness and the superiority of certain language varieties (Ferguson, 2009). Language policies can also be driven by de facto practices in the community, making them "subtle and hidden from the public eye" (Shohamy, 2006, p. 50). Thus, the scope and implications of LPP can be understood broadly to affect how people think about and use languages.

This notion of LPP is in line with Spolsky's (2004) framework to analyze language policies. The framework includes three components: language practices, language beliefs and ideology, and language management. These three components interact and overlap to shape language policy outcomes. The three components can be understood as:

- *Language practices:* individuals' habits and patterns of "selecting among the varieties that make up [their] linguistic repertoire" (Spolsky, 2004, p. 5). This includes the words, sounds, and grammatical features that individuals use in communication. Chapter 4 of this book will explore language practices in EMI classrooms in more detail.
- *Language beliefs and ideologies:* individuals' beliefs about language and how it is used. These beliefs are derived from and influence language practices. Teachers' and students' perceptions and beliefs about EMI will be explored in Chapter 5.
- *Language management:* explicit and direct efforts to control language through legal codification, statements, and documents produced by governments, institutions, and individuals. In its analysis of official language policies, this chapter explores the language management branch of Spolsky's (2004) framework.

Previous studies of EMI policies have noted that policy implementation varies according to geography (Costa & Coleman, 2012) and institutional identity

DOI: 10.4324/9781003202707-3

EMI policies in Turkey 19

(Doiz & Lasagabaster, 2017; Evans, 2008). This variation aligns with the notion of "policy arbiters," a term which recognizes the disproportionate influence that certain individuals have to enact policy even if they are removed from official policymaking processes (Johnson & Johnson, 2015). Research on language education policy has suggested that teachers often act as "the final arbiters of language policy implementation" (Menken, 2008, p. 5; see also Johnson, 2013) because of their influence in determining classroom practices. Other research on EMI policy has explored how national or institutional policies are "translated" into practice. For example, in complementary studies on EMI policy and its implementation in Japan, Rose and McKinley (2018) and Aizawa and Rose (2019) illustrate how national-level policy is interpreted at the institutional level and implemented at the classroom level. In a case study at a Malaysian university, Ali (2013) found that national-level EMI policy goals were not realized in institutional- or classroom-level practices. Specifically, through interviews with teachers, Ali (2013) found that EMI lecturers were unaware of how national-level policy aimed to improve students' English proficiency or of policy expectations for EMI classroom language use.

This chapter adds to our understanding of EMI policy by exploring national-level policies and their translation to the institutional level in Turkey. The following section presents key EMI policies in Turkey.

3.1 What are EMI policies in Turkey?

EMI policies at Turkish universities are regulated by Law No. 29662, "Regulations Concerning the Principles for Foreign Language Teaching and Teaching in a Foreign Language at Higher Education Institutions" (*Yükseköğretim Kurumlarında Yabancı Dil Öğretimi ve Yabancı Dille Öğretim Yapılmasında Uyulacak Esaslara İlişkin Yönetmelik*). This regulation was issued in the Official (National) Gazette on 23 March 2016 and replaced earlier directives under the same name. Evident from the name of the policy document, these national regulations refer to instruction in a foreign language or for foreign language education. Iterations of the directive date back to 1984, shortly after the founding of the Council of Higher Education (Yükseköğretim Kurulu, YÖK) in 1981 with the Higher Education Law (*Yükseköğretim Kanunu*, Decision No. 2547).

The directive establishes three types of medium of instruction (MoI) at Turkish universities: full instruction in a foreign language (*tamamen yabancı dilde eğitimi*), partial instruction in a foreign language (*kısmen yabancı dilde eğitimi*), and instruction in Turkish (*öğretim dili Türkçe*, TMI). In this chapter, these programs are referred to as full EMI, partial EMI, and TMI, respectively. The directive defines partial EMI programs as those in which at least 30% of the total degree credits are delivered through EMI. In other words, if students take ten equal credit-bearing classes in a partial EMI program, at least three of those ten classes must be taught in English (see Sahan, 2022, for more details on partial EMI programs). Although a legal distinction is made between full

20 EMI policies in Turkey

and partial EMI programs, the language proficiency requirements for staff and students, as well as admission processes, are the same for each form of education, as will be detailed in this chapter.

3.2 Analyzing policy: the ROAD-MAPPING framework

Having introduced the key national legislation, this chapter now uses the ROAD-MAPPING framework as an analytical tool to explore EMI policies in Turkey. The ROAD-MAPPING framework is a conceptual model that was developed by Dafouz and Smit (2016, 2020) to analyze language issues and the use of English in higher education against the backdrop of internationalization. The framework includes six dimensions: (1) roles of English, (2) academic disciplines, (3) management, (4) agents, (5) practices and processes, and (6) internationalization and glocalization. The ROAD-MAPPING framework captures the dynamic complexity of language policy in EMI settings by providing specificity for EMI research while remaining theoretically grounded in sociolinguistics and ecology of language (Dafouz & Smit, 2020). An illustration of the framework developed by Dafouz and Smit (2016) is reproduced in Figure 3.1.

Still in its early phases of development, the ROAD-MAPPING framework has been applied to a variety of contexts. It has been used to investigate stakeholders' beliefs or perceptions about EMI and to examine language use. The ROAD-MAPPING framework is robust enough to analyze EMI provisions at the country level (e.g., Bradford & Brown, 2017, in Japan; Kuteeva, 2019, in

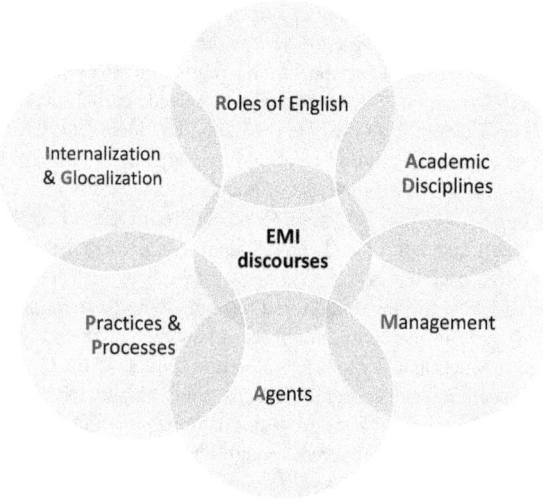

Figure 3.1 The ROAD-MAPPING framework (adapted from Dafouz & Smit, 2016)

Sweden) and to draw comparisons between contexts (e.g., Baker & Hüttner, 2017; Shao, 2019). In this chapter, the ROAD-MAPPING framework is applied to a new context and in a novel way: to analyze policy documents in Turkish higher education.

The next sections will present the findings from the analysis of EMI policies in Turkey using the ROAD-MAPPING framework. For the analysis, this chapter draws from a large study which collected data from seven universities to explore the variation with which EMI was implemented in Turkish higher education. A total of 145 national and institutional EMI policy documents were analyzed. In Turkey, education is regulated centrally, and national policy documents are issued by the Council of Higher Education (YÖK). National policy documents were accessed through YÖK and the national gazette (*Resmî Gazete*). Additional policy statements were accessed through newspaper publications. The institutional analysis examined EMI policies at seven universities, and the policy documents were accessed primarily from university websites for each of these seven universities. The universities included in this sample consisted of elite (n = 2), large (n = 3), and small (n = 2) institutions, and they are labeled accordingly (i.e., Elite-1, Small-1, etc.). The institutional policy documents included:

- Directive for Undergraduate Education (*Lisans Eğitim-Öğretim Yönetmeliği*);
- Promotion and Hiring Directive for Teaching Staff (*Öğretim Üyeliğine Yükseltilme Ve Atanma Yönergesi*);
- Annual Activity Reports (*Faaliyet Raporu*);
- Strategic Plans (*Stratejik Plan*); and
- Introductory Catalogs (*Tanıtım Kataloğu*).

Each university's website was also reviewed, including the website of its Engineering Faculty, the engineering departments included in this study, and its School of Foreign Languages (SFL). Policy documents were analyzed in *NVivo* using the ROAD-MAPPING framework as a deductive coding scheme, according to the procedures for qualitative content analysis (Selvi, 2020).

With its focus on EMI policy at both the national and institutional levels, this chapter aims to answer the following question:

What are the current national and institutional policies for EMI engineering programs in Turkey, and how do these EMI policies vary across universities?

In addressing this question, the chapter examines official EMI policies in Turkish higher education. The following sections are divided according to the six dimensions of the ROAD-MAPPING framework:

- Role of language (RO) refers to the function and status of English in relation to other languages in the multilingual university context;

22 EMI policies in Turkey

- Academic discipline (AD) considers EMI from the perspective of disciplinary knowledge and academic literacy;
- Management (M) refers to official regulations made by governing bodies concerning language use in the university context;
- Agents (A) considers the actors and agents involved in EMI;
- Practices and processes (PP) examines "ways of doing" and "ways of thinking" in EMI programs; and
- Internationalization and glocalization (ING) considers the motivations and constraints on universities to expand their global reach while also responding to the demands of the local context.

Within each section, the findings from national-level EMI policy documents are presented, and then EMI policies are compared across seven universities. These findings contextualize the EMI classroom practices presented in Chapter 4, and they complement findings on teachers' and students' perceptions of EMI policies presented in Chapter 5.

3.3 Role of English (RO) in EMI policies

This section addresses the role of English (RO) in relation to other languages in national and institutional EMI policy documents, beginning with the aims of EMI and English language teaching in Turkish HE. According to Article 5 of Law No. 29662, "the aim of instruction in a foreign language is to ensure that graduates of associate,[1] undergraduate, and graduate degree programs gain foreign language competences related to their fields" (Article 5, Law No. 29662). EMI instruction, therefore, has explicit language learning aims which are tied to the students' academic disciplines (ADs). This specific focus on language competencies with respect to academic discipline for EMI is in contrast to the aims of English language teaching:

> [T]he aim of foreign language instruction is to teach students the basic rules of the foreign language they are taking, develop their foreign language vocabulary, ensure that they are able to understand what they read and hear in the foreign language, and ensure that they are able to express themselves orally and in writing.
>
> (Article 5, Law No. 29662)

The aims of ELT/EFL classes, therefore, are more closely related to general English competencies rather than academic skills.

In addition to outlining learning aims, Law No. 29662 establishes the English preparatory program (EPP, or *hazırlık*) as a requirement for students enrolled in full and partial EMI programs, unless they meet the exemption criteria. Students enrolling in full or partial EMI programs must take an English proficiency exam, prepared by the HEI, at the beginning of the

EMI policies in Turkey 23

academic year. The proficiency exam determines whether students' English proficiency is sufficient to begin EMI classes. To gain exemption from the EPP, students must either:

(1) Pass the proficiency exam given by the HEI; or
(2) Have spent the last three years studying secondary school in a "native English-speaking country" (although the directive provides no definition of what it means to be a "native speaking" country); or
(3) Provide an English exam score from a national or international exam recognized by YÖK and meeting the English proficiency requirements set by the HEI.

Students who do not meet one of these criteria are enrolled to the EPP, the successful completion of which allows them to continue onto their EMI departmental courses.

Students who do not successfully complete the EPP may repeat it for an additional year, and students who have not met the English proficiency requirements within two years are removed from the EMI program. These students may then transfer to an equivalent TMI program.

Law No. 29662 also stipulates the English proficiency requirements for EMI lecturers in Article 8. EMI teachers must receive a score of at least 80% on a national English language exam (*Yabancı Dil Sınavı*, YDS), or the equivalent score on an international language exam, with equivalencies set by YÖK. Alternatively, they must have completed their studies or taught for at least one year at an Anglophone university or they must be "native" English speakers.

Thus, for both teachers and students, EMI language requirements are met by submitting exam scores or completing a period of study in an "English-speaking" country. Criteria for teachers also include work experience abroad, and students can meet the proficiency criteria by completing the EPP. However, while national policy establishes the EPP, it does not set a minimum proficiency requirement for EMI students. Instead, this is determined by individual universities.

To explore institutional policies, this study looked at seven universities. Table 3.1 provides an overview of the types of MoI programs offered at each of those universities. The table indicates whether *at least one* undergraduate program was offered for each MoI at the university.

At two of the universities, education was offered exclusively through EMI. The other HEIs offered education in a combination of EMI and TMI programs, and some offered programs taught through a different language (i.e., French literature taught in French or theology taught in Arabic).

In conjunction with its EMI programs, each university had an EPP, housed in the School of Foreign Languages (SFL), a separate unit of the HEI. The size and scope of the EPP varied according to the proportion of EMI programs

Table 3.1 Medium of instruction offered at HEIs

HEI	TMI	EMI		Other L2 MoI	
		Full	Partial	Full	Partial
Small-1	✓	✓			
Small-2	✓	✓	✓		
Elite-1		✓			
Elite-2		✓			
Large-1	✓	✓	✓		✓
Large-2	✓	✓	✓		✓
Large-3	✓	✓	✓		✓

Table 3.2 Language proficiency standards at each HEI

HEI	Internal exam	TOEFL IBT	IELTS	PTE Academic	YDS
Small-1	70	75	–	–	–
Small-2	70	78	–	67	65
Elite-1	60	79	6.5	–	–
Elite-2	60	75	6.0	55	–
Large-1	70	72	–	55	60
Large-2	70 (full EMI); 60 (partial EMI)	84 (full EMI); 72 (partial EMI)	–	71 (full EMI); 55 (partial EMI)	70 (full EMI); 60 (partial EMI)
Large-3	60	79	6.5	58	–

offered on campus. For example, at Large-2, approximately 5.5% of undergraduate students enrolled in the EPP (Large-2, Annual Activity Report); this percentage is small in comparison to the elite universities in which every undergraduate student was required to pass the EPP or meet its exemption criteria. At five of the universities, the SFLs also offered courses for other languages, most commonly German, French, and Arabic. However, English courses dominated the information available on SFL websites and information guides. For example, the mission statement of Large-3's SFL website specified aims for English learning but omitted other languages (e.g., Russian, German, French, Arabic) for which *hazırlık* education was offered.

At each HEI, an internal English proficiency exam was prepared by the SFL, and equivalency scores were set by the HEI for external exams. Table 3.2 compares the proficiency standards of students in EMI programs at each HEI. Generally, the HEIs required proficiency scores corresponding to about an intermediate level of English proficiency or B2 on the CEFR.

Large-2 sets separate proficiency standards for its full and partial EMI programs, requiring a higher passing score from students enrolled in full compared to partial EMI programs. Large-2 was the only HEI in the sample to do this.

Despite the proficiency standards indicated in Table 3.2, many of the institutional documents indicated concerns about students' English proficiency. One of the strategic aims listed in the Annual Activity Report of Elite-1 was to "develop students' command of the English language," including by developing "an atmosphere in which English can be used outside of the classroom throughout undergraduate education." While Elite-1's Strategic Plan included strategies to improve the EPP, it did not include strategies to support teachers and students engaged in EMI classes or to provide language support to administrative staff and nonacademic personnel. Elite-2 also identified English learning as an area for improvement, stating in its Strategic Plan: "Even though education is given in English, the foreign language proficiency of graduates is not as advanced as the level targeted." To improve the academic writing and speaking skills of students, Elite-2 called for "better communication between the SFL & departments to identify students' academic English needs" (Elite-2, Strategic Plan). However, the mechanisms by which coordination might occur were not identified in the report.

3.4 Academic disciplines (ADs) in EMI policies

This section addresses the second dimension of the ROAD-MAPPING framework: academic discipline (AD). From its analysis, this section concludes that English language learning is largely framed as separate and distinct from AD content learning in EMI policy documents.

References to AD in national policy documents are limited, in part because the directives address higher education broadly: the same policies regulate EMI for the natural sciences, social sciences, and humanities. References to AD are therefore generic, referring to students' academic field (*alan*), subject (*konu*), or vocation (*meslek*). However, national policies do not specify differences between ADs; for example, they do not state that *hazırlık* students should be separated by department or that the *hazırlık* curriculum should be prepared in line with discipline-specific language needs. Thus, *hazırlık*, in its implementation, is not necessarily AD-specific.

At the institutional level, the ADs most commonly taught through EMI at the seven universities were engineering, business, and international relations. The engineering departments at these seven HEIs were specifically examined: an examination of their engineering department websites revealed that EMI was often framed as advantageous for a career in engineering. The "Message from the Department Head" on the Mechanical Engineering Department's website emphasized the importance of EMI by stating:

> It has become exceptionally important in the competitive work life of our times that our graduates earn a prestigious diploma that is accepted in Europe and America. . . . We recommend that our youth apply to this prestigious [EMI] program in order to plan for a good career.
>
> (Small-2, Department website)

The RO and ING dimensions of the ROAD-MAPPING framework are also invoked in this statement to underscore the EMI department's assertion that English and an internationally recognized degree are necessary for mechanical engineers. Similarly, the Engineering Faculty of Elite-1 "deliver[s] programs with the aim of training youth who aim for engineering careers at an international level" (Elite-1, Annual Activity Report). This statement connects EMI and "international" engineering job opportunities (ING).

3.5 Management (M) in EMI policies

This section addresses the third dimension of the ROAD-MAPPING framework: language management (M). National policy documents primarily manage language education through the *hazırlık* program rather than describe academic study in EMI classes. YÖK has the authority to audit and terminate EMI programs, in which case the program would continue as a Turkish-medium program, and students would have the option of transferring to an EMI program at another university. Although Law No. 29662 gives YÖK the authority to audit EMI programs, the regulations do not specify how or through what processes YÖK carries out its monitoring responsibilities. Within an HEI, the university senate has the authority to establish EMI programs and criteria for language learning. The university senate establishes the *hazırlık* program and the conditions according to which English language proficieny exams are conducted. When considered from the perspective of management (M), the regulations thus specify by whom, to whom, and when an exam should be administered, and they mandate the creation of a *hazırlık* program for universities offering full or partial EMI programs. However, as noted in Section 3.3 (RO), the regulations do not provide additional guidelines concerning a minimum English proficiency standard for EMI students nor do they include provisions for continuous language support after *hazırlık*, when students are enrolled in EMI programs.

Institutional policies appeared to be similarly focused on the *hazirlik* program. To examine language management (M) in institutional documents, the analysis drew from two sources: each university's directives for teaching and learning published in the Official Gazette and their hiring and promotion criteria. The directives published in the Official Gazette established the *hazırlık* program within the SFL; however, additional information concerning language policies for teaching and learning in English was not provided. The language of assessment in EMI courses was mentioned in only one of the policy directives, that of Large-1, which stated: "Exams are also given in the foreign language for mandatory and elective classes taught through a foreign language" (Large-1, Official Gazette). In other words, it specified that the assessment for EMI courses should be in English. Similar statements were not found in the policy documents for the other institutions.

The institutional directives also included official language policy statements, which indicated the medium of instruction at the institution. In general, the universities' language policies consisted of two statements: first, they established the official language of instruction at the university; second, they outlined the conditions under which an alternative language of instruction may be used. For example, Large-3's language policy stated: "The language of instruction for classes is Turkish. However, for programs conducted in a foreign language the language of instruction is determined by the Senate." Elite-1's policy statement differed from this format in that it established English as the language of instruction but provided no clause for the use of Turkish-medium instruction. The official medium of instruction at four of the universities was Turkish (Small-2, Large-1, Large-2, Large-3), and English was the official language of instruction at two universities (Elite-1, Elite-2). Small-1's policy statement allowed for both English and Turkish to serve as official languages of instruction.

In addition to the directives published in the Official Gazette, the universities also regulated language policy through their hiring and promotion criteria. These criteria generally reflected national requirements for EMI teaching, although three of the universities (Small-1, Elite-1, and Elite-2) also required a demo lecture or seminar to be given in English. The purpose of the demo lecture was to evaluate the candidate's spoken English skills for teaching through EMI.

3.6 Agents (A) in EMI policies

This section addresses the fourth dimension of the ROAD-MAPPING framework: agents (A). The findings presented in this section demonstrate how macro-level actors (e.g., national agencies and university leadership) are framed as key decision-makers in national policy, while micro-level actors (e.g., teachers and students) are given less agency in decision-making processes for EMI programs. These national-level policies are replicated at the institutional level, where teachers and students appear to have limited agency in shaping EMI policies.

According to the regulations set forth in Law No. 29662, the three key actors in policy development are the university senates, rectorates, and YÖK. Key decisions concerning EMI policy are made by these three actors, including the decision to open an EMI program. In contrast, teachers and students follow or enact the regulations set by YÖK and the university leadership. For example, the task of arranging an English language proficiency exam for EMI students is the legal responsibility of the university rectorate, not language instructors in the SFL—although language instructors may carry this out in practice. Similarly, EMI department lecturers are absent from the English proficiency assessment process, despite their role as key stakeholders in understanding students' needs for EMI study. While the university senate might consult with or delegate responsibility to content and language instructors (i.e., by having the language instructors conduct the proficiency exam), there is no standard concerning how, to what extent, or in what capacity EMI teachers are included in EMI policy decisions. Further, while decisions concerning the English proficiency exam and the EPP are determined by universities, this is an institutional decision, not a departmental one. As such, the standards determined by the university might not be tailored to a specific program or academic discipline (AD). While teachers and students are not granted explicit avenues by which to shape EMI policy, they exercise agency as policy implementers in the classroom, as will be seen in Chapters 4 and 5.

The organizational structure of universities in Turkey is defined by national policy (i.e., Higher Education Law, Decision No. 2547). As such, there was little variation in the organizational structure of each of the seven universities examined in this study. Large-2 summarized its organization structure as follows: "[Large-2's] administration and organization is determined by the directives of Decision No. 2547. The administrative organs of the university are the Rector, the Assistant Rectors, the University Senate, and the University Administrative Council" (Large-2, Strategic Plan). Since HEIs were bound by national policies in terms of organization and leadership, the key decision-makers across the universities were those listed in national policy.

Similarly, decision-making with respect to admissions, hiring, and budgetary matters was largely controlled by YÖK, meaning that HEIs had limited flexibility in terms of establishing institutional policies. Elite-2 stated in its Strategic Plan that it would like to hire more international teaching staff but was hindered by national regulations:

> It is important that state universities like [Elite-2] with many international research and collaboration projects, a large number of international students, and at which the language of instruction is a foreign language employ international teaching staff. There are no problems in recruiting these staff positions. However, the provisions for International Teaching Personnel need to be revised. A report has been presented to YÖK concerning this matter.
>
> (Elite-2, Annual Activity Report)

The aforementioned statement regarding YÖK's role in the hiring process suggests that a tension exists between the aims of the HEI and national regulations for hiring international staff. Similarly, Large-2 noted in its Strategic Plan that it was limited in supporting international projects due to budgetary constraints set by YÖK (Large-2, Strategic Plan). These statements suggest that HEIs have limited agency in developing institutional identities or policy agendas due to national oversight. Nonetheless, decisions made at the departmental level shape the practices and procedures (PP) of EMI education, as illustrated in the following section.

3.7 Practices and processes (PP) in EMI policies

This section presents the fifth dimension of the ROAD-MAPPING framework, practices and processes (PP), which refers to "ways of doing" and "ways of thinking" in EMI programs. It includes activities related to teaching and learning in EMI classrooms. Because the analysis in this chapter is limited to explicit EMI policies in official policy documents, this section describes the PP of EMI envisioned by national policy; findings related to classroom practices are presented in Chapter 4.

Overall, regulations concerning PP were largely absent from national policy documents, which provided few guidelines for teaching academic content in EMI classrooms. Law No. 29662 includes only one provision that pertains directly to teaching and learning in EMI: Clause 14 of Article 8 states that exams, homework, and dissertation should be written in English. While this clause provides guidance in terms of which language should be used for EMI assessment, the regulations do not describe the language(s) that should be used in the classroom. Article 8(7) of the directive suggests that national policy might envision an implicit one-language-at-a-time form of instruction: "Classes that are given in a foreign language in higher education institutions will be given in this language by a lecturer who has command of the language." Here, the assumption appears to be that EMI classes will be conducted only in the foreign language. Further, partial EMI programs are defined with respect to course credits, with at least 30% of the total credits given through EMI (Law No. 29662, Article 4(1)(b)). In quantifying language use with respect to course credits, the directive appears to imply that each class should be conducted in only Turkish or English. Beyond this, the processes described in national policy documents do not offer guidelines for teaching and learning through EMI.

Similarly, the institutional policy documents did not offer specific teaching and learning guidelines. However, EMI departments were responsible for arranging their course curricula, such as by selecting the EMI classes offered in partial EMI programs and deciding on additional English courses to supplement the *hazırlık* program. Table 3.3 summarizes the arrangement of EMI and additional English courses in the EMI programs included in this study.

Table 3.3 Arrangement of courses in EMI programs

HEI	Engineering departments included in study	Full or partial	Arrangement of EMI courses	Additional English courses
Small-1	Civil	Full	Full	0
	Industrial	Full	Full	2
Small-2	Mechanical	Partial	Throughout	2
Elite-1	Mechanical	Full	Full	0
Elite-2	Mechanical	Full	Full	3
Large-1	Mechanical	Partial	Frontloaded	2
	Industrial	Partial	Throughout	3
Large-2	Environmental	Full	Full	2
Large-3	Mechanical	Both	Throughout	4
	Electrical	Partial	Throughout	4

30 *EMI policies in Turkey*

The findings presented in Table 3.3 were collected from department websites, course catalogs, and other department documents.

Partial EMI departments had some autonomy in determining which courses would be taught through EMI and how these courses would be distributed throughout the students' four years of study. The EMI component of the Mechanical Engineering program at Large-1 appeared "frontloaded" in that courses were arranged such that students took the majority of their EMI classes during the first two years of the program. The EMI courses required for the program were foundational courses in math and science (e.g., calculus, physics), which served as prerequisites for engineering classes (e.g., thermodynamics, heat transfer, hydraulics), the majority of which were taught through TMI. The only other EMI courses required in the program related to project management and laboratory work.

Although located in the same faculty as the Mechanical Engineering program, the Industrial Engineering program at Large-1 distributed EMI classes evenly throughout the students' four years of study. In the Industrial Engineering program, students took approximately two to three EMI courses per semester, including core engineering classes. Evident from the example of these two partial EMI programs at Large-1, the arrangement of EMI classes within partial EMI programs was determined at the departmental level, suggesting that EMI teachers and department heads had agency (A) in shaping the implementation of EMI programs.

In addition to determining *which* classes would be taught through EMI, departments with partial EMI programs also decided *how many* classes would be taught through EMI. For example, the partial EMI program in the Electrical Engineering Department at Large-1 exceeded the 30% minimum threshold: the department website reported that approximately 80% of courses were delivered through EMI, and students took more than four EMI courses per semester.

In terms of additional English courses included in the curriculum, differences were found across departments. For some EMI programs, students took a minimum of two semesters of English classes during the first year(s) of their program, typically EAP courses. At Large-3, students were required to take English classes during their first four semesters, consisting of two advanced English courses and two academic English courses. For other EMI programs, more English courses were built into the curriculum, including EAP courses and presentation skills courses. Thus, while national policy did not provide guidelines for teaching practices in EMI courses, individual departments had agency (A) in shaping their practices (PP) through the arrangement of the course curriculum.

3.8 Internationalization and glocalization (ING) in EMI policies

This section examines national and institutional EMI policies through the final dimension of the ROAD-MAPPING framework: internationalization and glocalization (ING). References to internationalization are largely absent from national policy documents. Law No. 29662 makes no reference to international students; instead, the regulations are primarily (although implicitly) directed at domestic students. For example, Law No. 29662 establishes the procedures by which a student who fails to meet the English language proficiency requirements can transfer to a TMI program. Here, the framing of Turkish as the default language of instruction for those without adequate English language proficiency implies that the regulation is primarily concerned with domestic students.

This orientation toward domestic students in national policy is reinforced in the university admission process, which is controlled centrally by YÖK in coordination with the national testing center (*Ölçme, Seçme Ve Yerleştirme Merkezi*, ÖSYM). These central governing bodies determine the allocation of students to university programs and set quotas for both domestic and international students at public universities. Thus, public HEIs, such as those included in this study, have little control over undergraduate admissions, limiting the university's potential to use EMI as a recruitment tool for international students.

At the institutional level, relatively few international staff and students were found in the EMI departments at the seven universities examined in this study. Only two engineering departments employed full-time international staff members, and at six of the departments, the number of full-time international students enrolled was less than ten (Small-1, Civil; Small-1, Industrial; Small-2, Elite-1, Large-2, Large-3, Mechanical). Nonetheless, the EMI programs offered opportunities for student mobility. Each of the HEIs included in this study offered Erasmus exchange programs for staff and students. Additionally, two of the Engineering Faculties at these universities included the option for a dual degree program with partner universities in the United States.

Although themes of internationalization appeared to various degrees in the mission and vision statements of the HEIs and their respective EMI departments, EMI rarely appeared alongside discourses of internationalization in institutional policy documents. Only Large-2 cited EMI as a strategy for attracting more international students (Large-2, Annual Activity Report). Otherwise, internationalization was described in terms of mobility and international rankings, without reference to EMI. For example, Small-1 and Small-2 listed increasing the number of international staff and students as strategic aims but did not reference EMI.

When English was mentioned within strategies for internationalization, it was often framed as a language of communication. In their Strategic Plans, Elite-2, Large-2, and Large-3 set the aim of maintaining English language versions of their HEI websites. In Elite-2's Strategic Plan, internationalization was tied to increasing English use on campus by "conducting every form of communication by academic units, administrative units, student clubs, etc., at the university in English" (Elite-2, Strategic Plan). Despite being a full EMI university, Elite-2 had identified the lack of communication in English as an obstacle to internationalization.

The universities also asserted local identities in their institutional documents. In its mission statement, Large-3 expressed pride in being a long-established university in Turkey, stating that it strived "to be a respected and leading university on the national and international stage" (Large-3, Annual Activity Report). Large-1 emphasized its ties to local industry, which it described as being important for graduates entering the job market (Large-1, Strategic Plan); many of these local companies had ties to global industry. As such, local (and glocal) identities were evident alongside discourses of internationalization.

3.9 Conclusion

This chapter has reviewed EMI policies at the national level in Turkey, and it has compared institutional EMI policies across seven universities. Its findings have highlighted a number of key aspects of EMI policies in Turkey.

At the national level, EMI policy is shaped by central government actors (A), which issue regulations governing HEIs across the country (M). National policies are primarily concerned with regulating English language proficiency and learning through the hazırlık program (RO). However, the regulations provide little direction or guidance for EMI implementation in departmental courses (M). While there is no proficiency requirement for admission to EMI programs, students who do not meet the English proficiency requirements of their universities are enrolled in hazırlık, a year-long intensive English language program designed to prepare students for EMI study (RO). As such, content and language learning are treated separately in national EMI policy documents, with language learning delegated to the hazırlık program rather than integrated into EMI departments (AD).

Thus, national policy provides provisions to support English learning before students begin their EMI programs (i.e., through hazırlık), but it does not specify additional language support mechanisms for staff and students *after* they have met the minimum requirements of English language proficiency for EMI. In other words, there is a tension between policy aims of English language learning *through* EMI and policy provision for English language support *before* EMI.

At the institutional level, policies established an official language of instruction for the university, English language proficiency requirements, and processes for hiring academic staff. EMI departments and the SFL were distinct academic units, thus separating content and language learning (AD). Content and language lecturers were removed from formal policymaking processes (M), since even at the institutional level, policy was largely determined by macro-level actors (A). These actors included national governmental agencies that regulated institutional-level decisions (M). However, EMI departments had an influence in shaping their EMI curricula (PP), especially in partial EMI programs, by deciding which classes and how many classes were offered through EMI. Furthermore, departments could require additional English classes as a means of ongoing language support to students (RO).

The seven universities whose policy documents were examined in this chapter varied in terms of the *amount* of EMI offered on campus (RO) and subjects offered through EMI (AD). They also varied in their arrangement of EMI program curricula (PP). The universities determined their own English language proficiency requirements for EMI students, and they required about a B2 level of proficiency according to the CEFR. Among the HEIs in the sample, only Elite-2's strategic documents suggested strategies to encourage collaboration between language instructors and content teachers. In general, institutional policies did not provide mechanisms to support the language needs of students and teachers involved in EMI content classes, after completing the *hazırlık* program or meeting the proficiency criteria.

Overall, EMI policy at both the national and institutional levels was found to be primarily concerned with English language learning through the *hazırlık* system, a prerequisite for EMI programs. Policies also did not provide guidelines for teaching and learning in EMI classes, other than to specify that classes should be taught in the target language by lecturers with the command of that language.

National and institutional policy documents did not appear to frame EMI as a strategy for internationalization (ING). National policies regulating admissions and hiring at state universities may limit the ability of HEIs to recruit international staff and students. This reflects the agency of macro-level actors (A) in controlling policymaking processes. However, department-level actors shaped the practices and processes (PP) of EMI programs by determining the course content and curriculum. The agency of content lecturers in shaping EMI practices is explored further in Chapter 4.

Note

1 Two-year degree programs (*önlisans*)

4 EMI classroom practices

With the expansion of English-medium instruction (EMI) worldwide, a number of studies have examined language use in EMI contexts typically focusing on approaches to teaching and learning (e.g., Lin, 2012) or the English language proficiency of students and lecturers (e.g., Jiang et al., 2019). Chapter 2 introduced research into EMI classroom practices in Turkey, noting that while early research relied primarily on teachers' and students' reported practices, recent studies have included classroom observations to explore how language is used in EMI classrooms. Some of this research has examined language use from the perspective of translanguaging, which "takes as its starting point language practices of bilingual people" (García & Wei, 2014, p. 22) and "leads us away from a focus on languages as distinct codes to a focus on the agency of individuals" (Creese & Blackledge, 2015, p. 26). This focus on the language practices and agency of bilingual speakers means that translanguaging sees multilingualism as a strength compared to monolingualism, for it multiplies a speaker's linguistic resources. Translanguaging sees the linguistic repertoires of individuals as a holistic basket of language resources and avoids using categories of named languages to segregate these resources. This understanding of language fluidity is evidenced in research on translanguaging in EMI settings worldwide (Paulsrud et al., 2021; Tai & Wei, 2021).

Beyond translanguaging, research examining EMI classroom practices has explored language choice in classroom interactions (Lo & Macaro, 2012; An et al., 2021), the types of questions asked by EMI teachers (Pun & Macaro, 2019), and the nature of L1 use (Söderlundh, 2013; Tarnopolsky & Goodman, 2014). In Sweden, Airey (2012) noted that EMI course materials were provided in English although lectures were often given in Swedish. Tarnopolsky and Goodman (2014) identified the primary functions of L1 use in EMI classrooms to be establishing rapport, disciplining students, and improving comprehension through explanations of content-specific terminology. This research suggests that codeswitching and L1 use are common phenomena which serve a variety of purposes in EMI classrooms. The findings presented in this chapter add to this body of research by exploring language use in EMI engineering classrooms in Turkey.

DOI: 10.4324/9781003202707-4

4.1 How are languages used in EMI classrooms?

This chapter draws on a larger study which collected classroom observation data from 21 EMI engineering classes across 7 Turkish universities. The universities consisted of elite (n = 2), large (n = 3), and small (n = 2) institutions, and they are labeled accordingly (i.e., Elite-1, Small-1, etc.). The 21 EMI teachers have been given identifying numbers for anonymity (i.e., Teacher 1, Teacher 2, etc.). The EMI lecturers were teaching undergraduate courses for engineering majors. The EMI lecturers were teaching in ten different engineering departments comprising five branches of engineering: mechanical, industrial, electrical, civil, and environmental engineering.

Each lecturer's class was observed twice, for a total of 85 lessons from the 21 EMI lecturers. This resulted in an average of four lessons per teacher. These lessons were typically arranged as blocks of two 45-minute lessons, which were observed on two separate days for a total of approximately three hours of observed classes per teacher. Nearly 68 hours of observation data were collected in total.

The observations were audio-recorded, and detailed fieldnotes were taken to mark additional information such as classroom dynamics, body language, visuals, or other materials used. After the data were collected, the recordings were transcribed for analysis in NVivo. The transcriptions included timestamps to correspond with the recordings; this enabled the analysis to include a time component to explore the proportion of class time for which teachers and students were engaged in specific language practices. Data were initially analyzed using a structured coding scheme which included categories of classroom language use, teacher- and student-talk, and language functions. The coding scheme was developed from the work of Tsui (1985) and adapted through piloting in the Turkish EMI context. Following the initial analysis of patterns in the data, the transcripts were explored in-depth to enable case study analyses of the observed EMI teaching practices.

Through its analysis of classroom observation data, this chapter aims to answer the following research question:

How are languages used in university-level EMI engineering classes in Turkey?

In addressing this research question, the chapter considers the functions of language use as well as practices which incorporate L1 use and translanguaging.

The following section presents key findings in terms of language use in the observed EMI classrooms. These findings describe patterns of language use in and across university-level EMI engineering classes. Next, the chapter highlights EMI classroom practices using case studies from the engineering teachers to illustrate variations of EMI implementation with respect to student participation and classroom language use.

4.2 What languages were used and by whom?

4.2.1 What languages were used?

First, data were analyzed according to language use in order to understand language preferences in EMI classrooms. The findings revealed that the EMI classes varied in the proportion of English used. On average, 56.42% of a lesson was conducted in English ($SD = 32.95$). However, while English accounted for 89.30% of one teacher's average lesson, no English-only utterances were recorded in two other teachers' classes. Still, English technical terminology appeared in these predominantly Turkish lessons through translanguaging and in written form to label figures on the board. This practice of translanguaging by using English terminology in Turkish utterances was fairly common; it accounted for an average of 8.18% of a lesson ($SD = 13.67$). Extract 4.1 provides an example of this type of translanguaging practice:

Extract 4.1

T: Buradaki temperature ve şuradaki temperature exactly aynı olmaz, bir taraf daha hızlıysa, yalnız şöyle oluyor. Temperature'lar yani voltajda olduğu gibi nolur, yani akıştada geçerlidir, bir taraf daha conductive iken bir taraf daha az conductive'ysa ısınma çoğu buradan gider, buradan birşey olur, ama gene temperature'ler balance eder. Buradaki assumption'lar.
[The temperature here and the temperature here won't be exactly the same, if on one side it's faster, actually it's like this. The temperatures, so what happens like it happens to the voltage? So it also happens with the current, if one side is more conductive and one side is less conductive, most of the heat is lost from here, something happens here, but still the temperatures will balance. These are the assumptions here.]
(T-10, Elite-1, Observation 1)

In Extract 4.1, the teacher used English terminology (*temperature, conductive, balance*) to explain the properties of heat transfer in Turkish. English terms, including less technical words such as "exactly," were also adopted into scientific explanations and incorporated into the grammatical structures of Turkish speech. For example, the teacher conjugated the English verb "balance" as a Turkish loanword (*balance eder*) and added the Turkish plural ending (*-lar/-ler*) to English terms such as "temperature" and "assumption." These flexible language practices are characteristic of translanguaging, and they were common throughout the observed lessons.

Just as the observed EMI classes varied in the proportion of English used, so too did they vary in Turkish use. Turkish-only utterances ranged from a maximum of 66.22% to a minimum of 0.96% of class time, with an average of 15.35% (SD = 19.55). When the translanguaging practices described in Extract 4.1 are included in these calculations, average Turkish use increases to approximately one-quarter of a lesson (M = 23.53%, SD = 29.90), with the highest proportion of Turkish use (including translanguaging practices) recorded as 82.12% of class time. These results suggest that, while some EMI lessons were conducted almost entirely in English, others were carried out almost entirely in Turkish with English terminology appearing to discuss scientific topics.

4.2.2 Who was talking?

Next, patterns of interaction were investigated to explore what proportion of class time consisted of teacher-talk and student-talk. The findings revealed that teacher-talk accounted for the largest proportion of the EMI lessons (M = 62.38%; SD = 17.15). Teacher-student interaction was found to range from 5% to 45% of a lesson (M = 20.66%, SD = 11.67). In addition to teacher-talk and teacher–student interaction, pauses were found to account for 15.93% (SD = 8.78) of class time on average. These "pauses" included periods during which no one was speaking as part of the lesson; often, teachers were drawing diagrams or figures on the board during these pauses. Finally, student-talk independent from teacher-student interaction accounted for less than 1% of the lessons on average (M = 0.81%, SD = 1.38), and this was found to be relatively consistent throughout the dataset. Low proportions of student-talk occurred because the lessons were structured as teacher-centered lectures with few opportunities for pair or group work or other student-centered activities. These findings indicate that the majority of EMI classes offered limited opportunities for student output in English, although relatively higher proportions of teacher-student interaction were observed in some classes (as will be discussed in Case Study 1).

4.2.3 Who was using what language?

Finally, these analyses were combined to explore what languages were used by whom. In other words, what language(s) did teachers and students typically use during the observed EMI classes? To do so, the number of utterances by a speaker according to language (e.g., the number of utterances in English by teachers) was analyzed. The findings indicated that the majority of teacher-talk occurred in English, accounting for 78% of utterances in the dataset. The remaining approximately 20% of teacher utterances included Turkish-only utterance as well as Turkish utterances with translanguaging (as shown in Extract 4.1).

While teacher-talk primarily occurred in English, no single language accounted for the majority of utterances in teacher-student interaction:

approximately 40% of teacher-student interaction sequences occurred in English-only, 30% in Turkish-only, and the remaining 30% of utterances occurred in a mix of Turkish and English (e.g., were characterized by some form of translanguaging). These translanguaging interactions often involved students speaking in Turkish and their teacher responding in English, as in Extract 4.2:

Extract 4.2

T: So you will have ten days, enough time to do the homework. You will be using computer-aided tools. Solid works and atoms, for homework three, alright?
S1: Başka bir yazılım kullanabiliyor muyuz?
 [*Are we able to use another computer program?*]
S2: Kaç tane soru? [*How many questions?*]
S3: Başka bir yazılım—[*Another computer program*–]
T: Hm?
S1: Başka bir—[*Another*–]
S3: Başka bir yazılım kullanabiliyor muyuz? [*Are we able to use another computer program?*]
T: Which one, for example?
S3: [name of software]
T: Huh?
S3: [repeats name of software]
T: I think it should be fine as long as uh you feel comfortable and if the corrections, the uh answer is correct.

(T-9, Elite-1, Observation 2)

Here, the students asked questions related to their homework assignment in Turkish while the teacher responded in English. Interactions consisting of translanguaging practices commonly occurred in this manner, with students speaking Turkish and the teacher responding in English. Taken together, these findings suggest that, overall, the EMI teachers primarily spoke in English and that Turkish was relatively more common for teacher-student interaction than it was for teacher-talk.

4.3 For what purposes were these languages used?

Having explored patterns of language use in the observed EMI classes, the analysis then focused on the functions of language use to understand what purposes English and Turkish—as well as translanguaging—served. The aim of this analysis was to explore whether different languages (Turkish, English) served different purposes in the EMI classrooms. The most common functions of language use are presented in Table 4.1, which shows the average

Table 4.1 Most common functions of language in EMI classrooms (percentage of class time)

Rank	Function	Proportion	Frequency
		% of class time across classroom averages $M\ (SD)$	Times appearing per class $M\ (SD)$
1	Present or explain new content	50.09 (13.28)	53.06 (16.32)
2	Ask question related to content	16.45 (7.83)	28.31 (18.01)
3	Pause	15.93 (8.78)	45.05 (23.83)
4	Provide "off-content" information related to the course	5.61 (2.81)	9.30 (4.40)
5	Explain, clarify, or summarize the presented content	2.96 (1.54)	3.43 (2.28)
6	Give math-based example to explain or apply concept	1.75 (1.64)	2.97 (4.56)
7	Introduce new content or concepts	1.54 (0.76)	4.43 (2.85)
8	Give instructions or procedural commands	1.19 (1.40)	2.75 (2.77)
9	Give daily-life example to explain or apply concept	1.11 (1.44)	1.03 (1.05)
10	Check student comprehension	1.01 (0.80)	5.16 (3.96)

proportion and frequency with which each function occurred in the EMI lessons.

The most common function identified in the data was "present or explain new content," which accounted for about half of each lesson (M = 50.09%, SD = 13.28). The next most common language function was "ask (or answer) questions related to content" (M = 16.45%, SD = 7.83). "Pauses" accounted for 15.93% (SD = 8.78) of class time on average, and "provide 'off-content' information related to the course" comprised 5.61% (SD = 2.81) of the lesson. The majority of an average lesson appears therefore to have been spent on the presentation and discussion of content material.

Table 4.2 shows the most common functions found for each language category. What emerges from the findings is not only that each language category served a variety of pedagogical purposes, but also that the same main functions were found across language categories.

English was predominantly used to "present or explain new content" (50.27%); it was also commonly used to "ask questions related to content" (20.53%) as well as to "provide 'off content' information" (5.88%). Turkish was used for similar purposes: to "present or explain new content" (33.94%), "ask questions related to content" (25.18%), and "provide 'off-content' information" (15.97%). Thus, when comparing the functions of English and Turkish utterances, both languages were primarily used to present and ask questions related to academic content.

Table 4.2 Functions by language according to frequency and percentage of coding

Function	English only (L2)		Inter-sentential L1/L2		Intra-sentential L1-L2		Turkish only (L1)	
	f	%	f	%	f	%	f	%
Present or explain new content	3316	50.27	62	12.58	341	50.82	612	33.94
Ask question related to content	1354	20.53	290	58.82	185	27.57	454	25.18
Provide "off-content" information related to the course	388	5.88	48	9.74	39	5.81	288	15.97
Check student comprehension	313	4.75	9	1.83	13	1.94	86	4.77
Introduce new content or concepts	296	4.49	6	1.22	15	2.24	49	2.72
Explain, clarify, or summarize the presented content	190	2.88	8	1.62	28	4.17	58	3.22
Give instructions or procedural commands	144	2.18	5	1.01	8	1.19	65	3.61
Translate technical vocabulary	4	0.06	23	4.67	29	4.32	4	0.22

To understand the functions of translanguaging, these utterances were divided into two categories: inter-sentential L1/L2 use and intra-sentential L1/L2 use. Although the paradigm of translanguaging aims to move beyond static categories of named languages (i.e., L1 and L2), these categories served functional and practical purposes in this study by allowing us to compare patterns of language use. Inter-sentential L1/L2 use referred to examples of language mixing at the sentence level, whereby a sentence was uttered in one language, and then the next sentence was uttered in another (e.g., the mixed languages interactions in Extract 4.2), whereas intra-sentential L1/L2 use referred to practices of language mixing within sentences (e.g., inserting English words into Turkish utterances in Extract 4.1).

Inter-sentential L1/L2 use most commonly occurred to "ask questions related to content" (58.82%), such as during exchanges between teachers and students (again, see Extract 4.2). It was also used to "present or explain new content" (12.58%), such as by providing simultaneous translation. However, the translation of technical terminology occurred infrequently in the EMI lectures, with the function "translate technical vocabulary" appearing 73 times in total in the dataset or less than once per lesson ($M = 0.86$ times per lesson). Thus, inter-sentential translanguaging was generally not used for direct translation.

Intra-sentential L1/L2 use occurred more frequently in the dataset than inter-sentential L1/L2 use, and it was most commonly used to "present or explain new content" (50.82%). These practices involved Turkish explanations of academic content with English technical terms (again, see Extract 4.1). Intra-sentential translanguaging was also used to "ask questions related to content" (27.57%), with teachers and students constructing their utterances in Turkish but using English technical terminology. Thus, the classroom observation data has revealed that translanguaging was primarily used for pedagogical purposes directly related to teaching and learning—specifically, to present and ask questions about academic content. These findings also match the main functions of language use identified for English-only and Turkish-only utterances, suggesting that these different languages served similar functions in the observed EMI classes.

4.4 Case studies

To summarize the findings from the classroom observation data presented so far:

- Language use varied across classrooms, with some EMI classes taught predominantly in English and others using more Turkish and/or translanguaging practices;
- The lectures tended to be teacher-centered, although the amount of teacher-student interaction varied across classrooms;

42 EMI classroom practices

- In the dataset as a whole, the majority of teacher-talk occurred in English, while teacher-student interactions were likely to take place in Turkish and include translanguaging practices;
- The three most common functions of language use were "present or explain new content," "ask questions related to content," and "provide 'off content' information related to the course." These functions were found to be the top three functions across languages.

These findings have revealed important themes with respect to language use and teacher-student participation. Translanguaging was a common practice in EMI engineering classes, and it was primarily used to present and discuss academic content. However, student participation in English occurred relatively infrequently in the observed EMI lessons. This suggests that EMI classroom practices might not be assisting in the realization of EMI's supposed dual aims. In other words, if students are not provided with opportunities for output in English, the development of their English communicative skills through EMI might be limited.

To further explore these themes with respect to student participation (in English) and translanguaging practices in EMI engineering classes, the following sections present two case studies. The first case study highlights techniques used by two teachers to encourage student participation in English; and the second case study highlights the language practices of one teacher, with specific focus on language awareness and translanguaging.

4.4.1 Case study 1: interactive lessons in English

Our first case study focuses on teaching practices that contributed to the implementation of interactive lessons in English. This case study describes EMI classrooms which were primarily conducted in English and in which relatively high levels of teacher-student interaction were observed. The case study comprises two parts: the first part of the case study will focus on Teacher 16, who taught Environmental Engineering at a large university, and the second part will focus on Teacher 6, who taught Mechanical Engineering at a small university. Together, these case studies allow us to explore practices that encouraged student participation in English in EMI classes.

To increase student involvement, resulting in higher proportions of teacher-student interaction, Teacher 16 worked to scaffold language and content through the use of simple, often close-ended questions. In a semi-structured interview after the observation, he explained that this approach to EMI teaching allowed him to cope with low levels of student English proficiency and to ensure that the students were engaged in the lesson. In practice, this meant that the teacher created opportunities for students to participate in class in English, even if only through one- or two-word responses. The teacher structured his lectures to include a high number of low-order thinking questions which required short responses from students. While this limited the complexity of student output, it also contributed to a relatively high number of student utterances in English. An example of such questioning throughout the lecture is provided in Extract 4.3, which comes from a fourth-year Water Treatment course.

Extract 4.3

T: Manganese?
  <pause, 3 seconds>
T: Okay. Tell me about the oxidation states.
S1: There's the two plus, and the four plus.
T: Manganese plus two.
S1: And the four plus.
T: Plus, manganese four plus. Okay. Which one is more soluble? Four plus? Two plus?
S1: Two plus
  <Ss call out answers>
T: Two plus is more soluble. What about four plus?
S2: Less soluble.
T: Less soluble. So what is the product here? Manganese?
S3: Oxide.
T: Dioxide. It is the solid form, okay? So we have black?
Ss: Sludge
T: Sludge.
  <writing, pause, 4 seconds>
T: Just like ferrous iron, in the treatment of manganese, as long as it is in two plus oxidation state, what do we, what do we have to do? The main treatment is to? Go from here to here. So oxidation.

(T-16, Large-2, Observation 2)

In this example, the teacher engaged students in questioning, activating their existing schema and encouraging them to participate in the lecture. Although students responded to the teacher's prompts, the questions asked by the teacher were simple ("*Which one is more soluble?*"), and student output was minimal ("*two plus*"), typically consisting of one- or two-word answers. Through this style of questioning, the linguistic burden on students with lower levels of L2 English proficiency was decreased both in terms of output and input, as teacher-talk was typically limited to short questions or explanations, rather than lengthy monologues in English.

Teacher 16 also used question prompts to assess student comprehension and to provide additional explanations, such as explanations of technical terms in English. Teacher 16 frequently checked students' comprehension of vocabulary and technical terms—at least in comparison to other EMI teachers in the sample—suggesting that he was more inclined to focus on students' comprehension of terminology in English. An example of vocabulary checking is provided in Extract 4.4.

Extract 4.4

    T: What about trace ionic species? Trace?
    S: Ionic species?
    T: Trace? Trace, the. Trace means, trace meaning they are found in wa— in surface and sub-surface water but at very low concentrations. Okay? Trace mean, okay.

                                      (T-16, Large-2, Observation 1)

This extract is taken from Teacher 16's fourth-year Water Treatment course. Here, the teacher checked student comprehension of the word "trace" by repeating it as a question. When the students provided no indication that they understood the meaning of the word, the teacher explained its meaning in English rather than provide a Turkish translation (see Case Study 2 for comparison). In doing so, the teacher maintained English as the medium of instruction.

In Teacher 16's classes, high levels of teacher-student interaction in English were made possible by the teacher incorporating frequent questions and opportunities for students to participate in class. His questions were simple, which decreased linguistic challenges for students. While this limited the complexity of student output, this style of teaching encouraged students to participate in class, provided the teacher with a mechanism to ensure that students were following the lecture, and reasserted English as the primary medium of instruction. Nonetheless, a reliance on low-order thinking questions raises concerns about the depth and quality of student learning.

In contrast to the questioning strategies used by Teacher 16, Teacher 6 encouraged student participation in English in his EMI classes by asking students to present short summaries of the previous lecture at the beginning of each taught session. Student presentations, summaries, and explanations were uncommon in the EMI engineering classes, which made Teacher 6's lessons unique. At the beginning of the lesson, Teacher 6 selected a student to summarize the key concepts covered in the previous lesson. Extract 4.5 provides an example of a student summary from this teacher's class:

Extract 4.5

    S: Okay. Hi. My name is Yusuf,[1] and I'm gonna recap last week's lesson. Uh. We started to examine the vectors and first of all we, uh we determined the magnitude of the resultant vector uh x [=*TR*] as a thermal, x [=*TR*] and y axis. <writing> For example, we have like this force and uh we have to determine the uh equal–

T: Determine! <corrects pronunciation>
S: Determine. We have to determine the components of this force. Uh. As a form of x [=TR] and y axis. And uh how can we uh how we can do this? Uh we specify the, this angle and for example thirty degrees. And uh we <writing> we completed this at the head of the force vector uh. Y and x [=TR] axis. And we draw this, and this is F-x [=TR]. It is called F-y, and we can, uh we can find out this uh by doing this equation.

(T-6, Small-2, Observation 1)

This extract provides an example of extended student-talk in English, which occurred because the student was asked to present a "recap" of the previous week's session. Extended student-talk was relatively rare in the observed EMI classes. In this instance, it allowed the student to draw upon his knowledge of academic presentation skills in English: the student began by introducing himself and framing the topic of his presentation (*"Hi. My name is Yusuf, and I'm gonna recap last week's lesson"*). The student also used the chalkboard as a resource for multimodal presentation, as he wrote the vector equation on the board to assist in his explanation. In the focus group discussion for this class, students reported that they prepared notes for the recap presentations in advance, in case they were called on by the teacher to present. In contrast to the student output observed in Teacher 16's class, this student in Teacher 6's class provided a lengthy, multi-sentence response; however, his response contained little evidence of higher-order thinking, since the student's recap primarily summarized an example provided by the teacher in the previous lesson. This practice of drawing on previously presented examples was confirmed by students in the focus group, in which students indicated that their preparation relied on copying or memorizing specific examples from their lecture notes.

Although the recap provided an opportunity for extended student-talk, the teacher interrupted the student's summary to ask questions and provide additional information. In Extract 4.5, the teacher corrected the student's pronunciation of the word "determine." He did not, however, comment on the student's pronunciation of the letter "x" in Turkish. Teacher 6's explicit feedback with respect to the pronunciation of "determine" reflects the importance that this teacher attributed to accuracy in English, which the teacher summarized in an interview after the observed lesson by stating, *"there's a difference between accent and pronunciation. Our students need to be understood"* (T-6, Small-2, interview 2). Similar examples of EMI teachers correcting their students' pronunciation in English were rare throughout the dataset, as other teachers tended not to comment on their students' output in English.

Both Teacher 6 and Teacher 16 described their motivation for using these practices as a desire to build students' confidence in English. Teacher 6 stated: *"They're nervous to speak in class, so I try to encourage them to do that. That's why I have one student summarize in English at the beginning of the class*" (T-6, Small-2, interview 2). Similarly, Teacher 16 explained that he used questions throughout his lecture in order "*to encourage them to speak, yeah, to respond to my questions. . . . Otherwise, they sit there and just listen, and some of them, they fall asleep*" (T-16, Large-2, interview 2). Together, the examples taken from Teacher 16 and Teacher 6 represent techniques used to encourage students' participation in English.

These case studies have illustrated the strengths and weaknesses of these techniques. In the case of Teacher 16, short questions were used to elicit responses from students. Although the student responses were generally limited to one- or two-word answers, the questioning technique encouraged students to engage with the lesson. Teacher 6 asked students to provide recaps of key concepts, which encouraged students to produce longer utterances in English and provided them with opportunities to practice their presentation skills, including through the use of multimodal presentation styles such as writing on the chalkboard. These techniques are notable in terms of scaffolding student participation in English, and they resulted in higher levels of student participation compared to other lessons observed in the sample. However, the effectiveness of these techniques in terms of contributing to students' higher-order thinking skills and in-depth engagement with academic content is limited. The questions asked by Teacher 16 were lower-order thinking questions, raising concerns about the depth of student learning, and the students in Teacher 6's class reported memorizing examples from their notes for the recap. Together, these examples represent initial steps in scaffolding to support student participation in EMI; however, they suggest that EMI teachers may benefit from pedagogical training to support higher-order thinking.

4.4.2 Case study 2: English preparation, Turkish discussion

Our second case study centers on the language practices observed in Teacher 18's class in the Mechanical Engineering Department of a large university. The aim of this case study is to highlight the translanguaging practices used by Teacher 18. While examples of translanguaging have been highlighted earlier in this chapter (i.e., Extracts 4.1 and 4.2), the language practices used by Teacher 18 in his EMI class were distinct because of the roles that Turkish and English played in the presentation and discussion of academic content.

Teacher 18's class was initially identified as a unique case in the sample because a much higher proportion of pauses were found relative to other classes (44.1%, compared to an overall average of 15.9%). In terms of proportion of language use, a higher proportion of Turkish (including Turkish with English lexical items) and a lower proportion of English use were also found in Teacher 18's lessons, compared to overall averages. As will be seen, the language practices observed in this EMI class can be described as using prepared language in English and conducting spontaneous discussion in Turkish. Teacher 18 presented prepared texts in English, such as by reading paragraphs from slides or lecture notes. Then, following the recitation of these English texts, he discussed the content in Turkish, such as by providing a Turkish summary or eliciting student questions. The high proportion of pauses found in this class resulted from the teacher copying his English lecture notes onto the board for students to write in their notebooks. When asked about these language practices, Teacher 18 described his English language proficiency to be insufficient for EMI lecturing—making him the only teacher in the sample to have self-reported language challenges. When asked to describe his language use in the class, the teacher said he was "*not ready yet*" to teach in English (*T-18, Large-3, interview 1*). Therefore, he used the board and other visuals such as writing, diagrams, and slides to facilitate EMI teaching. Visuals and diagrams "*make it easier . . . Because sometimes, I don't have to explain in English because [the students] see what's going on, on the board*" (*T-18, Large-3, interview 2*). In practice, this meant that Teacher 18 often read directly from his slides and copied his notes verbatim, reducing the amount of spontaneous speech in English. The teacher rarely deviated from his preplanned notes, which were supplemented by Turkish explanations and summaries to clarify meaning. Students asked questions most often in Turkish, and Teacher 6 usually replied in Turkish. The teacher's style of presenting new content first from his prepared notes in English followed by a Turkish explanation is illustrated in Extract 4.6, from a second-year Strength of Materials course.

Extract 4.6

T: Negative. It means that point D moves to the left or right?
S1: Left
S2: Left
T: Left.
   <writing, pause 38 seconds; T writes: "*This negative result indicates that point D moves to the left.*">
T: Uhm, this is displacement d. It means, displacement of point D with respect to a. It's actually delta d slash a. Okay, but when second point x is a fixed point, generally we don't use the fixed point's name.
   <writing, pause 8 seconds>
T: For the displacement of point B, relative to point C, what will you say? For the beginning? B and for C.
   <writing, pause 7 seconds>
T: This is the relative displacement. B to C. With respect to C.
   <writing, pause 53 seconds; T writes, "*Here the negative sign indicates that B will move toward C.*">
T: Sadece bu termin b ile c'in arasındaki, b'in, c'ye göre yerdeğişimi negatif, birbirine yaklaşıyorlar demek.
   [*Just this term is going to be between b and c. The displacement of b with respect to c is negative, so it means they're getting closer.*]
   <writing, pause 4 seconds>

48 EMI classroom practices

T: Böyle bir c belki sağa gidiyor ama b, daha fazla sağa gidiyor, dolayısıyla ne olmuş oldu? İkisinde birbirine yaklaşmış oldu, o yüzden bu relatif, evet kelimesi önemli.
[*Maybe C is going to the right like this, but then B is going further to the right, therefore what happens? They end up approaching each other, so this is relative, yes this word is important.*]
(T-18, Large-3, Observation 1)

Here, the teacher showed the students how to solve a problem related to axial loading by writing full English sentences on the board, at one point including a 53-second pause to copy down an English sentence from his notes. In this way, the teacher ensured that what he had written on the board was not only scientifically accurate but also grammatically correct. For Teacher 18, texts, diagrams, and visuals facilitated EMI teaching by reducing the linguistic demands of lecturing in English.

As the English used in these lectures was largely preplanned, the teacher frequently highlighted aspects of the language written on the board. In addition to summarizing in Turkish, the teacher drew attention to specific English words that were critical to understanding the course content or which he thought the students were less likely to know. This is illustrated in Extracts 4.7 and 4.8, respectively, in which the teacher provided a Turkish translation of the word "arbitrary" and an explanation of the word "yield":

Extract 4.7

T: <*reading*> Using the method sections the differential elements of the length d-x. And cross sectional area a of x. Is isolated from the bar at arbitrary position. <*reading ends*> Arbitrary? What's the meaning? Arbitrary position. Rastgele. [*Random*] <*reading*> Where the modulus of elasticity is e of x. The free body diagram is shown in figure d.
(Teacher 18, Large-3, Observation 1)

Extract 4.8

T: İçindeki çıkartıyoruz, değil mi? O tüp şekilde çünkü.
[*We're taking about the inside, right? Because it's shaped like a tube.*]
<pause, 10 seconds; T writes: "Solving Eq (1) and (2) simultaneously yields F−a−i = 30 N, F−b−i = 15 N">

T: Bu *yeilds* kelimesi, bu tars kullanıldığı zaman denklem bir ve ikinin aynı anda çözümünden, bu çıkartma gibi bir anlamı geliyor, malzemedeki *yield*, bakma anlamındaki değil bu.
[*This word* yields, *when it's used like this, from solving equation one and two at the same time, it means something like this is the solution. Don't look at the* yield *from materials, that's not the meaning of this.*]
(Teacher 18, Large-3, Observation 3)

In both of these examples, the lexical item explained by the teacher was encountered in English materials used during the lesson. In Extract 4.7, Teacher 18 came across the word "arbitrary" while reading a text to the students. He paused to check whether the students had understood the word. Deciding that they had not—based on the lack of response from the students—the teacher then provided a Turkish translation ("*rastgele*"). Although the teacher provides a direct translation of the term here, direct translation was relatively uncommon across the EMI classes observed for this study (see Section 4.3). In Extract 4.8, the teacher copied a sentence onto the board which contained the word "yield." The teacher then explained, in Turkish, how this use of the word "yield" differed from other usages students had previously encountered in their EMI studies ("*the* yield *from materials*"). Through these explanations, the teacher focused on English terminology found in materials used to present the academic content.

As illustrated in this case study, Teacher 18 incorporated visual aids (e.g., writing on the board) and prepared texts to assist with content instruction. The English used to teach was preplanned, and the L1 was used for summaries and discussions of the English lecture notes. While this slowed down the pace of the lecture by adding more "pauses" in class, it provided opportunities to focus on the English used in academic contexts, which may have afforded scaffolding opportunities to students. Nonetheless, this case study raises concerns about the effectiveness of EMI teaching in this style, particularly with respect to the teacher's confidence using English and the lack of spontaneous discussion in English. While this case study highlights Teacher 18's innovative translanguaging practices to overcome his own language challenges, it raises concerns about EMI teachers' linguistic preparedness and the support available to them. It also illustrates how students may have limited opportunities to develop their academic and communicative English skills if discussion opportunities are not provided in English.

4.5 Conclusion

The findings presented in this chapter have revealed that the EMI engineering courses in Turkey are neither English-only nor English-always in their implementation, although EMI classroom practices vary. The analysis of classroom observation data has focused on patterns of classroom interaction. Interaction is considered to be an important component of good teaching pedagogy because the degree to which students are actively involved in their lessons may have an effect on both content learning and language development (Morton, 2012). In fact, teacher-student interaction has been described as "the most significant pedagogical resource that contributes to learning" (Macaro, 2018, p. 187). As illustrated in Case Study 1, some EMI teachers used innovative techniques to encourage participation, although questions remain as to the depth of student engagement with academic content and the effectiveness of these techniques for supporting higher-order thinking. As seen in Case Study 2, interaction was often achieved through the use of Turkish.

This chapter has also demonstrated that classroom language practices varied within and across institutions according to language choice and speaker talk time. This variation was particularly noticeable with respect to differences in L1 use and the amount of teacher-student interaction found in the classrooms (see Sahan et al., 2021, for more on L1 use and interaction). The case studies provided in this chapter have illustrated this variation with respect to teaching practices that encourage student participation—questioning and student summaries—as well as the ways in which multilingual practices were used to present and discuss academic content. These multilingual practices represent teachers' and students' language choices for classroom teaching, and they reflect the de-facto language policies of EMI classes (compared to the official language policies explored in Chapter 3). As illustrated through the extracts shared in this chapter, language use was often characterized by flexible translanguaging practices. Moreover, Case Study 2 presented an example of translanguaging instruction, with English lecture notes and Turkish discussions. The teacher used preplanned lecture notes, slides, and texts to teach in English, and he supplemented these with Turkish explanations to enhance both the teacher's and students' ability to overcome linguistic challenges and engage with the academic content. Still, the effectiveness of these practices for building confident, bilingual engineers remains questionable, and the case studies have suggested that EMI teachers may benefit from the ongoing linguistic and pedagogical support.

That EMI education is implemented differently across university contexts and between classes within the same department has implications for the quality of education and learning outcomes. The EMI classes described in this chapter are regulated by the same national EMI policies (see Chapter 3). However, the language practices observed in these lessons varied, with implications for students' linguistic and academic development. Considering the variation with which EMI was implemented in these university classes, the following chapter examines teachers' and students' perceptions of EMI for teaching and learning in engineering programs, respectively.

Note

1 Pseudonym has been used.

5 Teacher and student perceptions

Having explored English-medium instruction (EMI) policy and practice in Chapters 3 and 4, this chapter examines teachers' and students' perceptions of EMI for undergraduate engineering programs in Turkey. Previous research on EMI has examined stakeholders' beliefs through survey data (Costa & Coleman, 2012; Kırkgöz, 2014; Macaro & Akincioglu, 2018) and interviews (Baker & Hüttner, 2017; Dafouz et al., 2016). Research on stakeholders' perceptions has covered a range of topics including the benefits and challenges of EMI. Specifically in Turkey, these studies have found that students generally believe that EMI is beneficial for their English language skills, although they report language challenges associated with EMI (e.g., Dearden & Akincioglu, 2016). Lecturers in Turkey have similarly been found to identify challenges associated with teaching academic content through English (e.g., Başıbek et al., 2014).

Of relevance to this book, previous research on teachers' and students' perceptions of EMI has explored teachers' perceptions of L1 use in class (Lasagabaster, 2017) and students' views of their EMI teachers' language use (Macaro, Tian, et al., 2018). In the latter of these studies, the authors concluded that "on the whole students wanted their lessons to be predominantly in English but that when comprehension problems did occur they were open to the idea of Chinese being used" (Macaro, Tian, et al., 2018, p. 13). Similar findings were reported from a study looking at EMI programs in Vietnam and Thailand: Sahan et al. (2022) report that teachers and students held "mixed views" on L1 use in class, with many participants expressing a preference for English-only EMI while also acknowledging the pedagogical benefits of L1 use. As Chapter 4 demonstrated that the L1 was commonly used in EMI engineering classes, this chapter will explore students' and teachers' perceptions of language use.

Research has also looked at teachers' perceptions of their identity as EMI teachers (e.g., Airey, 2012; Dafouz et al., 2016; Moncada-Comas & Block, 2019). On the whole, these studies have found that teachers primarily see themselves as responsible for conveying subject knowledge, not for developing students' English language skills. The findings from these studies may offer insight into why EMI teaching practices are found lacking focus-on-form instruction or teaching which promotes language learning. Building on the diverse studies cited earlier, this chapter explores in depth the perceptions of teachers and students engaged in EMI teaching and learning on undergraduate engineering programs in Turkey.

5.1 What do teachers and students think about EMI?

It is important to understand teachers' and students' perceptions of EMI, because they are the key stakeholders involved in its micro-level implementation. As such, the ways in which teachers and students conceptualize EMI policy and practice are likely to influence the ways in which academic content is taught through English in classrooms, as well as the ways in which teachers and students respond to challenges. This chapter draws from a larger study investigating EMI implementation in Turkey in order to explore teachers' and students' perceptions of EMI policy and practice. These findings complement the themes discussed in Chapter 3 and Chapter 4 by foregrounding teachers' and students' voices.

The data presented in this chapter are sourced from the analysis of semi-structured interviews with 21 EMI teachers, including stimulated recall interviews, and 25 focus group discussions with EMI students (150 students in total). Each teacher was interviewed twice, for a total of 42 interviews. The 21 lecturers interviewed for this study were the same teachers who participated in the classroom observations (Chapter 4), and the interviews were conducted after each classroom observation. The students, who were enrolled in the teachers' EMI classes, were invited to participate in the focus groups following the second classroom observation. The students were predominantly male (male = 110, female = 40), reflecting the tendency for engineering programs to enroll more male than female students. The vast majority of the students were local Turkish students, with only five international students participating in the focus groups. This reflects the low number of international students enrolled in the observed courses. All interviews and focus groups were recorded and transcribed for analysis in *NVivo* using qualitative content analysis for emerging themes (Selvi, 2020).

The participants included in this study came from seven state universities in four cities. The universities included elite (n = 2), large (n = 3), and small (n = 2) institutions, and they are labeled accordingly (i.e., Elite-1, Small-1, etc.). When the participants are quoted or referenced in this chapter, they are given an identifying number (i.e., Teacher 1 is T-1, Teacher 2 is T-2, etc.) along with university information, to protect the participants' identities while also providing sufficient context to interpret the findings.

The findings presented in this chapter answer the following question:

How do teachers and students perceive EMI in university-level engineering programs in Turkey?

The following sections will explore teachers' and students' perceptions of:

- EMI policy, with specific focus on policy implementation and the English language proficiency requirements for EMI programs;
- Students' linguistic preparedness for EMI, looking at the quality of English language education and the *hazirlik* program in Turkey; and
- Classroom practices, specifically the use of English, Turkish, and mathematics in EMI engineering education.

These findings build upon those presented in Chapter 3 and Chapter 4 to offer further insights into EMI policies and practices in Turkish higher education.

5.2 How do teachers and students understand EMI policy?

Building on the findings from Chapter 3, this section explores teachers' and students' perceptions of EMI policies, policy inconsistencies, and English proficiency requirements.

5.2.1 Official EMI policy

When asked to describe official EMI policy, or what is written in policy documents, both teachers and students described EMI policy as English-only instruction. However, they also believed that there were no repercussions for lecturing in Turkish rather than English. Teacher 5 summarized official policy for full and partial EMI programs as follows:

> Now it's like this, 30 percent English does not mean this, in our classes it's not 30 percent English and 70 percent Turkish. Some classes are entirely English, and some classes are entirely Turkish. . . . But of course, we have to give the classes that are English in the curriculum in English, and the Turkish classes in Turkish. In the 100 percent English program, the whole curriculum is English.
>
> (T-5, Small-2, interview 1)

Teacher 5's explanation of EMI policy indicated that one language should be used at a time (i.e., "entirely English" or "entirely Turkish") and that the language of instruction was predetermined according to the course curriculum.

Other teachers also noted that EMI policy envisioned one-language-at-a-time instruction: "the university policy is all classes are in English, that's it" (T-11, Elite-2, interview 2). However, teachers also emphasized that this policy was not enforced in practice. Teacher 20 explained, "The classes are supposed to be either English or Turkish but in practice we use both" (T-20, Large-3, interview 1). Thus, although teachers perceived EMI policy to envision English-only instruction, they also recognized that EMI practices diverged from this—a theme which will be picked up in the following section on EMI classroom practices.

According to teachers, one reason for the divergence between policy and practice was the lack of clear repercussions for violating the English-only policy. Teacher 21, who was the head of the Electrical Engineering Department at his university, described the limitations with enforcing EMI language policy:

> Just last week, a complaint came from a foreign student in one class from the 30 percent program. He says the teacher speaks Turkish and he wants this class in English. . . . So I told the teacher to teach in English. But he has two sections of this class, and he asked, "What should I do?" So I told him to teach one in English and one in Turkish and the students can go to the Turkish section if they prefer. But then the students started complaining that their section was in English and the other was in Turkish. . . . So in the end, I told the teacher to teach both in English.
>
> (T-21, Large-3, interview 2)

Here, Teacher 21 highlights the complexity of language policy in practice. Following a complaint about Turkish use in an EMI class, Teacher 21 sought a resolution that satisfied both Turkish and international students. Notably, he mentioned no consequences for the teacher lecturing in Turkish. In general, teachers perceived no form of institutional oversight or punishment for violating EMI policy.

In the absence of an enforcement mechanism, both teachers and students perceived classroom language practices to be more fluid and bilingual than envisioned by official policy. In every focus group (n = 25), students stated that classroom language use was determined by the teacher. They described teachers who used Turkish as "relaxed" in terms of adhering to EMI policy, and they contrasted them with teachers who were "strict" in following the "rules" (i.e., only using English to teach). One student summarized, "the teacher might, if he or she is a relaxed person, sometimes go to Turkish and not return to English" (Student 2, T-8, Elite-1). Nonetheless, both teachers and students expressed frustration with what they perceived to be inconsistencies with EMI policy implementation, elaborated on next.

5.2.2 Inconsistencies in EMI policy

As noted in the previous section, the implementation of EMI policy was viewed to be more flexible than envisioned by official regulations, and students described teachers as "relaxed" or "strict" depending on their adherence to English-only policies. Because of this variability between teachers, students perceived three types of inconsistencies in EMI policy implementation:

1. *Inconsistencies within an individual teacher's class*: students expressed frustration at the inconsistency with which teachers allowed students to ask questions in Turkish. They reported that teachers sometimes enforced an English-only policy by requiring students to speak in English but other times allowed L1 Turkish use. One student described:

> [T]he thing that makes me upset there, look, what are people doing? I'm saying [in Turkish], teacher can I ask a question? She's saying, English please. But someone else goes directly into Turkish, and she doesn't warn them, she just lets them continue.
> (Student 4, T-16, Large-2)

2. *Inconsistencies across classes:* Students reported variations in language policies by different teachers, as well as in different classes taught by the same teacher. They stated: "One explains in English, one explains in Turkish" (Student 3, T-6, Small-2); "Last semester, he taught a class and it was all in English, but this one is all in Turkish" (Student 4, T-21, Large-3).
3. *Inconsistencies between lectures and exams:* students perceived a lack of consistency in language expectations for lectures and exams: "some of the teachers teach in Turkish, like you saw. But the exams are in English, the exams are always in English" (Student 1, T-2, Small-1). Students highlighted the difficulties that this inconsistency created for them in terms of understanding exam questions in English, particularly when they had not been exposed to English terminology during lectures.

Teachers also perceived inconsistencies with EMI policy, although the issues that they described occurred at the institutional level. For example, Teacher 21 perceived his EMI department to be limited in its ability to formulate a coherent language policy, because YÖK controlled the admissions process for international students (Chapter 3). This teacher stated that it might be best if international students were only admitted to full (not partial) EMI programs, but "we don't even know [international students] have been accepted; they just show up. All of that, the application, and the acceptance, and their assignment here, it's all done by the Council of Higher Education" (T-21, Large-3, interview 1). Similarly, Teacher 15 noted limitations in the department's ability to establish L2 proficiency criteria for its Master's program:

> For our Master's program our department [wants to] require a minimum of like 65 or 70 on the language exam. And when we send this request to the university, the Senate, they say, we don't require a language score. So it's just open to everybody. But we teach in English.
> (T-15, Large-1, interview 2)

In each of these cases, teachers perceived limitations in their departments' ability to formulate coherent EMI policies due to constraints imposed by more macro-level actors.

5.2.3 Policy requirements for L2 proficiency

In addition to inconsistencies in EMI policy implementation, teachers and students also perceived issues with the policy standards for L2 proficiency. Specifically, they did not perceive policy—which requires students to pass the *hazırlık* program as a prerequisite for EMI study—as stipulating a clear, minimum level of L2 proficiency. Students in one focus group (FG, T-3, Small-1) stated that they were required to achieve a B2 level of English proficiency before enrolling in their EMI classes. This was the only focus group in which students provided a specific, minimum level of L2 proficiency. However, the students expressed skepticism that the minimum passing grade from the EPP corresponded to a B2 level of proficiency: "If you meet the necessary standards, you pass the proficiency [test] and whatever. If you don't pass, you take the course and you need to reach B2. That's what it's called here but it's actually intermediate" (Student 3, T-3, Small-1). These students were unable to articulate what they perceived as the difference between B2 and "intermediate," although they did elaborate on the shortcomings of their linguistic preparation: "the English we saw in *hazırlık* and the English we see in the department are not the same" (Student 2, T-3, Small-1). Teacher 21 also cited B2 as the target level of L2 proficiency necessary for EMI study, although he noted that, in practice, the EPP "get[s] students] to B1 and assume[s] they'll learn the rest here" (T-21, Large-3, interview 2). Aside from these participants, the other teachers and students did not report knowing the level of English proficiency to which completion of the EPP corresponded.

In contrast to the vagueness with which they perceived L2 proficiency requirements for students (e.g., pass *hazırlık*), teachers described in detail the L2 proficiency requirements for teaching in EMI. Teachers reported two means through which lecturers could meet the L2 proficiency criteria: teachers must either receive a score of at least 80 points on a national language exam or have completed their PhD studies abroad (see Chapter 3). One teacher summarized:

> Not just anyone can teach in English; it's not just about whether you want to teach in English. You need to meet certain requirements. There are two ways you can meet these requirements. One, you can get a certain score on an exam, on an English exam. So either on YDS or an international exam, you get a certain score. Or two, you have an international degree. You get your degree from an international university.
>
> (T-19, Large-3, interview 1)

Other teachers noted that their departments added additional criteria for EMI teaching because the national exam (*YDS*) did not include a speaking component. For example, some teachers stated that their departments encouraged applicants to submit TOEFL scores instead, since the TOEFL exam included speaking assessment. Many of the teachers saw the national exam as insufficient for measuring their linguistic prepared to teach through English because of its emphasis on grammar. Some of the teachers' comments are summarized as follows:

- "It says nothing about how well you can teach. Solving grammar on a test is not like teaching [in English]" (T-19, Large-3, interview 1).
- "Someone looks at my exam score and says, okay you can teach in English, but no one checks to see if I can speak English" (T-7, Small-2, interview 1).

Teacher 21 (Large-3, interview 1) also noted that teaching skills and pedagogical training were absent from policy requirements. He stated that language proficiency alone did not qualify one as a competent teacher: "just because you get a certain score doesn't mean you can teach in English. These are different skills" (T-21, Large-3, interview 1). Moreover, he noted that teaching ability is not the main criteria considered during the university hiring process, since universities value an applicant's research record more than his or her teaching ability. Teacher 21's statements are supported by the lack of teacher training offered to EMI lecturers: of the 21 lecturers included in this study, only two had received any kind of pedagogical training (T-6, Small-2 & T-14, Large-1), and both received this training during their PhD studies in the United States.

5.3 How do teachers and students perceive the students' English language education?

This section explores participants' perceptions of students' linguistic preparedness for EMI courses. To explore this theme, we investigate teachers' and students' perceptions of the quality of English language education in secondary schools and *hazırlık*.

5.3.1 Quality of English education in secondary schools

Students and teachers perceived issues regarding students' linguistic preparedness for EMI. Both teachers and students were critical of the English language teaching (ELT) curriculum provided in secondary schools through the National Ministry of Education (*Milli Eğitim Bakanlığı*, MEB). The MEB curriculum introduces ELT classes in primary school, meaning that most students received eight years of English instruction before entering university.

58 Teacher and student perceptions

However, participants perceived students to enter university with little or no knowledge of English due to the low quality of ELT classes in secondary schools; this meant that the one-year intensive EPP was insufficient for preparing students for EMI study. Students in one focus group stated:

S2: The problem is with MEB. We started learning English in the fourth grade but somehow still could not learn it properly.
S1: Yeah, the problem starts in elementary school. I mean, we studied for eight years before we came here but we never learned anything. Even now, we have trouble speaking.

(FG, T-8, Elite-1)

Among the perceived issues that resulted in students having "never learned anything" was the emphasis on grammar teaching in the MEB curriculum: across focus groups, students stated that they only studied grammar in their English classes throughout primary and secondary school. Students also noted that the ELT curriculum was repetitive and slow-paced: "The things that we learned in the elementary level of *hazırlık* were the same things that we saw for four years [in high school]" (Student 2, T-6, Small-2). Teachers (e.g., T-18, Large-3, interview 1; T-5, Small-2, interview 1) also perceived that the MEB curriculum's emphasis on grammar limited effective language learning.

In one focus group, students noted that their classmates who came from rural areas were less prepared linguistically than students from urban centers like Istanbul: "It's like they meet English when they come [to university]. So they have no background with English. They still have some problems getting used to English and I don't think [the EPP] is enough" (Student 3, T-8, Elite-1). The student quoted here—who graduated from an elite EMI high school in Istanbul—perceived that some students were less linguistically prepared for EMI than others because of their secondary school experiences. Similarly, one teacher stated:

This is a state university, so we get students from all different backgrounds. Especially the ones who study *hazırlık*, they come in with a very low level of English and they only get one year of instruction in the *hazırlık*. I don't think it's enough.

(T-11, Elite-2, interview 1)

In explaining why she perceived *hazırlık* to be insufficient, Teacher 11 noted that many students entered university "with a very low level of English" due to the quality of English language education in their secondary schools. These comments raise concerns about the equity of English language education at secondary schools in Turkey.

5.3.2 Quality of the English preparatory program

The findings presented in the previous section highlighted perceived issues with the quality of English education in secondary schools. As was reported in that section, many participants perceived that the EPP was "not enough" because students entered university with very low levels of English proficiency. This section examines the perceptions of L2 English learning in the EPP.

Students in many focus groups (e.g., FG, T-8, Elite-1; FG, T-5, Small-2; FG, T-6, Small-2; FG, T-9, Elite-1) were pleased with the quality of their *hazırlık* education, but they perceived that the one-year intensive program was insufficient for EMI study. Students in other focus groups were less satisfied with the quality of their EPP, which they perceived as oriented toward grammar teaching (e.g., FG, T-17, Large-2; FG, T-19, Large-3); these students reported that the EPP had not adequately prepared them for the linguistic demands of EMI. Student perceptions of the effectiveness of the EPP varied across universities, suggesting that some *hazırlık* programs may be more rigorous than others.

In terms of weaknesses in the EPP curriculum, some students pointed to an emphasis on grammar teaching, which they believed hindered the development of their speaking skills. They also reported difficulty understanding technical vocabulary because it was not taught in *hazırlık* (e.g., FG, T-5, Small-2; FG, T-9, Elite-1; FG, T-4, Small-2; FG, T-3, Small-1). The following quotations from students summarize these concerns with *hazırlık*:

- "We know the past perfect but we can't speak. I mean, we can't use it so there's no point in knowing the rule" (Student 4, FG3, T-14, Large-1).
- In [the English] preparation school, we didn't learn anything about the mechanical terms, we just learned English grammar, so when we came to the department, it's really not—I mean, it's different, there's a difference between the English at prep year and the English we use here.

(Student 8, T-11, Elite-2)

Many teachers (e.g., T-1, Small-1, interview 1; T-14, Large-1, interview 2; T-15, Large-1, interview 1; T-11, Elite-2, interview 1; T-19, Large-3, interview 1) also perceived the EPP to be insufficient for preparing students for EMI study. These teachers believed that some of their students had language challenges due to low English proficiency.

In order to address issues with the quality of the EPP, Teacher 16 stated that he was working with language teachers to revise the curriculum:

We are working with [the director of the EPP] to improve the English education. The first two years, it was bad, because the *hazırlık* wasn't ready.

60 *Teacher and student perceptions*

> But we've been working with [the director] . . . so I hope the students' English is getting better.
>
> (T-16, Large-2, interview 1)

Teacher 17, who lectured in the same department, confirmed Teacher 16's account of collaboration with language teachers (T-17, Large 2, interview 1). However, they were the only teachers in the sample to report collaborating with language instructors. Teacher 21 stated that he had wanted to work with teachers in the *hazırlık* program to improve the quality of English education but was unable to do so for logistical reasons:

> We don't know exactly what they do over there [in *hazırlık*]. We're trying to change the structure of the *hazırlık* program to give students a better education. But, you know, they have their own limitations and their own problems, you know, with class sizes or desks or teaching hours, or I don't know, they have their own needs, so we can't just tell them to change it.
>
> (T-21, Large-3, interview 2)

Teacher 21 perceived the structure of the university to deter collaboration with colleagues teaching in the EPP, since language teachers had their own "limitations and problems."

5.4 How do teachers and students understand EMI classroom practices?

As Chapter 4 demonstrated that EMI teaching practices varied in terms of language use and students' participation, this section explores teachers' and students' perceptions of EMI classroom practices.

5.4.1 *Use of English in EMI classes*

Only one teacher perceived no challenges resulting from the use of English to teach academic content in her course. This teacher explained: "I think they are pretty capable of following what's going on and our preparatory English class during the first year is pretty good" (T-8, Elite-1, interview 1). The remaining 20 teachers in the sample, however, described language-related challenges resulting from English use. Teacher 11 explained why she perceived students to struggle with English in her EMI courses:

> [Students] come to me after class or during break times to ask questions. And of course we're speaking Turkish then, but the questions they're asking, they're things I've said multiple times during the lecture. So I think they don't understand because of the language, because when I explain it in Turkish, they're like, "oh!"
>
> (T-11, Elite-2, interview 1)

Because of the perception that students struggled to understand content in English, many teachers stated that they incorporated Turkish into their lectures—a theme which will be discussed in more detail in the following section.

Because of these language challenges, students perceived the clarity of their teachers' English explanations as particularly important because "*one unknown word comes and we've lost the flow of the lecture*" (Student 3, T-6, Small-2). Another student estimated that she understood less than half of what was taught in class: "*I don't think I have much knowledge because it is in English. I mean, if it were in Turkish, it would sink in more. [In EMI], we understand 30 percent, 40 percent of the course*" (Student 6, T-16, Large-2). As such, some students noted that it was easier to understand teachers who adjusted their lecturing style in English, such as by speaking slowly:

S3: I really like this teacher because he speaks slow and repeats.
S4: He explains everything step by step. I mean, if it were in Turkish, he wouldn't explain it like this, but he does this so it's easy for us to understand [in English].
S3: Yeah, if a teacher speaks too fast, we cannot understand.

(FG, T-17, Large-2)

Similarly, other students (e.g., FG1 and FG5, T-14, Large-1; FG, T-15, Large-1) believed that their teachers modified their spoken English to increase student comprehension: "Our teacher adjusts his language for us, so we can understand better. I mean, he uses more basic words, like he uses more daily life language than scientific language, to make it easier for us to understand" (Student 6, FG5, T-14, Large-1). Thus, students perceived some teachers as accommodating their English to enhance student comprehension.

However, other students were less likely to describe their teachers' English use positively. Instead, they criticized their teachers' English proficiency or accent, as illustrated in the following quotes:

- "I don't want to criticize too much, but I don't think that [some] teachers' level of English is high enough to teach in English" (Student 1, T-9, Elite-1).
- "We have teachers who speak a lot better, especially the ones who spent more time in America" Student 2, T-15, Large-1).
- "Everyone has a bit of their own pronunciation style. When [pronunciation] changes from teacher to teacher we get confused" (Student 3, T-20, Large-3).

Many participants also perceived English as a barrier to student participation in EMI classes. Students across focus groups stated that they had difficulty asking questions in English and lacked confidence speaking English. One student stated: "When [the class] is English, participation really drops" (Student 1, T-7, Small-2). Many teachers allowed students to ask questions in Turkish because they believed that it was better for students to participate in Turkish than not participate at all. One teacher stated: "at the beginning of the semester I told them, you know, ask your questions in English. But I don't enforce that because then they don't ask anything" (T-13, Elite-2, interview 1). Many teachers agreed, noting that students:

- "Have trouble when they ask questions, when they express themselves in English" (T-17, Large-2, interview 1);
- "Cannot give full answers in English" (T-16, Large 2, interview 1); and
- "Don't trust their English" (T-14, Large-1, interview 2).

Some teachers sought to address the low levels of student participation by encouraging students to speak English in class (see Case Study 1 in Chapter 4). For example, Teacher 6 states: "They're nervous to speak in class, so I try to encourage them to do that. That's why I have one student summarize in English at the beginning of the class" (T-6, Small-2, interview 2). Teacher 6 incorporated student summaries in his lessons to provide students with opportunities to practice speaking English. Similarly, Teacher 16 asked questions to students throughout his lecture in order "to encourage them to speak, yeah, to respond to my questions. Otherwise, they sit there and just listen, and some of them, they fall asleep" (T-16, Large-2, interview 2). Teacher 7, however, perceived motivation to play a role in students' willingness to speak English: "That kid in the back who kept participating, he wants this; he wants to speak English. Some kids want to take English classes, and some kids are the exact opposite and don't want to take English classes" (T-7, Small-2, interview 1). Similarly, teachers also perceived a number of nonlinguistic factors that contributed to low student participation. These factors included:

- Poor attendance;
- Personality;
- Difficulty of course content;
- The time of the class;
- Gender dynamics; and
- Class size.

Furthermore, some teachers noted that they had similar issues regarding student participation in both Turkish and English. Teacher 1 noted that student participation was low, even though he taught his EMI class in Turkish (Chapter 5): "I'm speaking Turkish but it's still like this. If it were in English, participation would be zero" (T-1, Small-1, interview 1). As such, although teachers perceived the use of English to affect student participation, they did not perceive the language as the only factor contributing to low student participation in EMI classes.

Nonetheless, students stated that it was easier to formulate questions in Turkish than in English, particularly when content was difficult: "sometimes we are seeing really complicated things, and when you are trying to ask really complicated questions, confusing things, to the teacher, it's really hard to explain in English" (Student 2, T-8, Elite-1). Students in one focus group stated that it was the "mindset" of the students which prevented them from asking questions in English: "people just feel more comfortable with Turkish, I think. So they just don't challenge themselves to really improve their English" (Student 2, T-9, Elite-1). Another student in the same focus group stated that the "speaking part is kind of hard to get used to, speaking in English. Because our teachers are Turkish, and you're Turkish, and so you speak in Turkish" (Student 3, T-9, Elite-1). In this focus group, the students noted that Turkish was an easy default, because it was a common language shared by students and teachers.

These comments from both teachers and students demonstrate how they perceived L1 use from a deficit view: they saw Turkish as a resource used to overcome language-related challenges in English. This view stands in contrast to the scholarship on translanguaging practices, which has highlighted language fluidity as a natural part of bilingual practices. While the participants in this study seemed to have embraced translanguaging practices—or the fluid use of multilingual resources in the classroom—they do not seem to have embraced a translanguaging ideology, which would move away from this deficit understanding of L1 use. This theme is explored further in the following section on teachers' and students' perceptions of L1 Turkish use.

5.4.2 Use of Turkish in EMI classes

The previous section examined students' and teachers' perceptions of English use in EMI courses. As seen in the previous section, teachers and students believed that (some) students struggled to understand academic content taught in English and that Turkish use could facilitate comprehension. The previous section concluded by noting that Turkish use was framed by participants in deficit terms, who described it as necessary because of low English proficiency. This section delves more deeply into these perceptions, and it compares teachers' and students' views on the use of L1 Turkish in the classroom.

In general, teachers and students perceived that it was appropriate for teachers to use Turkish to clarify concepts that students did not understand or were having difficulty understanding in English. The majority of teachers (n = 14) stated that they used Turkish in class to explain concepts that students did not understand in English. Still, seven teachers reported that they did not use Turkish to clarify content during lectures. Among the teachers who did use Turkish, they perceived it to be a natural linguistic resource in the classroom. Teacher 5 criticized strict English-only policies, stating: "The person listening to the lecture is Turkish, and the person giving the lecture is Turkish, so it starts to turn into a theatrical production" if Turkish is forbidden (T-5, Small-2, interview 1). Similarly, Teacher 19 stated, "you can use only English in class, but if the students do not understand you, this is not teaching; this is talking. . . . You are just talking to yourself" (T-19, Large-3, interview 1). He stated that teachers have an obligation to teach students "even if their English is not good enough. We need to teach them as well" (T-19, Large-3, interview 2). In order to teach students with low English proficiency, many teachers believed that "sometimes Turkish support is necessary to make sure they understand why and what's happening" (T-18, Large-3, interview 2). Many students also shared their teachers' perception that using Turkish made the lecture easier to understand (e.g., FG, T-3, Small-1; FG, T-7, Small-2; FG, T-19, Large-3), and some students stated that their teachers' use of Turkish helped them focus during lectures (FG, T-20, Large-3).

However, some teachers (e.g., T-11, Elite-2, interview 2; T-12, Elite-2, interview 2) believed that it was not appropriate to use Turkish, especially if an international student were present. Teacher 12 stated that he would only respond to students in Turkish

> [I]f there is no foreign student and if the question is in Turkish and if it is not directly related to the content of the course . . . but the core of the course has to be taught in English. You cannot use another language.
>
> (T-12, Elite-2, interview 2)

Another teacher stated that he rarely used Turkish in class because it was easier for him to explain scientific concepts in English: "I think it's easier for me to explain things in English. If I have to explain it in Turkish, I still use English words" (T-9, Elite-1, interview 2).

Only one teacher perceived issues with his own English proficiency as a reason for using Turkish in class. Teacher 18 stated that his "aim is pure, hundred percent English" during the lecture but that he is "not ready yet" to lecture only in English (T-18, Large-3, interview 1; see Case Study 2 in Chapter 4). Here, the teacher stated that his English proficiency prevented him lecturing entirely in English. Teacher 18 was the only teacher to express concerns with his English proficiency.

With respect to the presence of international students in the classroom, Teacher 11 stated that it was "unethical" to use Turkish if an international student were in the class (T-11, Elite-2, interview 2). This perception was not shared by all teachers in the sample, some of whom used Turkish with international students in their EMI classes. Teacher 1 and Teacher 2 both claimed that the international students in their classes were proficient in Turkish: "I have two foreign students in the class, but they both speak Turkish so it isn't a problem. They've been in Turkey for a while" (T-2, Small-1, interview 2). However, the two international students from Teacher 2's class stated in a focus group that they would understand the content better if the teacher lectured in English rather than Turkish: "Yeah, I learned Turkish, but I still wish the class were in English. That'd be better" (Student 2, T-2, Small-1). International students also reported that they felt socially isolated on campus, at least initially, because student clubs and other social activities were primarily conducted in Turkish (FG, T-16, Large-2; FG, T-8, Elite-1). Thus, regardless of teachers' preferences for language use in EMI classrooms, international students appeared to perceive linguistic barriers arising from Turkish use on campus.

Although Teacher 11 stated that it would be "unethical" to use Turkish in an EMI class when international students were present, she also perceived that it was useful to allow students to ask questions in Turkish:

> It's a balancing point. You know, if I enforce [an English-only policy] too much, they're going to say just—I'm sure it happened before, I mean, they're just going to say, "no it's fine, I'm not asking. I'll ask it after the class." So I don't want to prevent them from asking. . . . My goal is not to make them speak English. It's just that they understand thermodynamics.
> (T-11, Elite-2, interview 2)

Teacher 11 perceived content learning—not language learning—as the primary aim of her EMI classes. As such, she allowed students to ask questions in Turkish during the class. The "balancing point" described by Teacher 11 reflects the attitudes of other teachers and students toward the pedagogical benefits of L1 in EMI classes, and it reflects the flexibility with which EMI policy is implemented.

5.5 Conclusion

This chapter has explored teachers' and students' perceptions of EMI policies and practices at Turkish universities. With respect to EMI policy, teachers and students perceived variations in policy implementation but no repercussions for violating official EMI policy. Students described classroom-level policy implementation as determined by the teacher, who could be "relaxed" or "strict" about English-only policy. Teachers perceived inconsistencies in EMI policy and criticized the lack of a speaking proficiency requirement for lecturers.

Participants perceived language challenges, particularly around understanding lectures and speaking English in class. However, they did not perceive these challenges in isolation from the broader education system of Turkey. Rather, participants reported issues with the secondary school system, which resulted in low student L2 proficiency and overburdened *hazırlık*. To overcome these language challenges, teachers and students saw Turkish as a useful resource for teaching and learning. However, participants differed in their perceptions of how, when, and by whom Turkish should be used in EMI classes. While these findings demonstrate an openness to translanguaging practices, they raise doubts as to whether participants have embraced a translanguaging ideology which moves beyond deficit thinking of L1 use.

6 Conclusion

This book has explored English-medium instruction (EMI) policies, practices, and perceptions in Turkish higher education. Chapter 1 introduced key concepts in relation to EMI, and Chapter 2 explored research on EMI in Turkish higher education. Chapters 3, 4, and 5 then presented the findings from a large-scale study investigating EMI policies, practices, and perceptions in undergraduate engineering programs at seven Turkish universities. This final chapter discusses those findings in relation to relevant theory and empirical research on EMI in Turkey and elsewhere.

In comparing policies, practices, and perceptions of EMI in Turkey, this chapter argues that the role of English in EMI is multifaceted and complex. This chapter is organized around four themes, which synthesize the findings from the previous chapters: EMI implementation, English proficiency and linguistic preparedness, L1 Turkish use, and the theoretical dual aims of EMI. Each of these themes contributes to an understanding of the variation with which EMI is implemented in university classrooms in Turkey.

6.1 EMI implementation

Turkey is unique compared to many other EMI contexts in that there is a formal, top-down policymaking process with respect to university regulations. This process was explored in Chapter 3, which argued that language and content teaching are separated in EMI policy in Turkey. Still, despite the presence of central guiding policies in Turkey, this book found great variation in the amount of English used in the EMI lectures. This finding with respect to variation in L2 use concurs with previous findings from other contexts (such as secondary schools in Hong Kong, e.g., Lo & Macaro, 2012; Pun & Macaro, 2019) and supports the results of other studies, which have found that—regardless of policy intentions—the norms of language use in EMI classrooms are constructed by teachers and students (e.g., Kerklaan et al., 2008; Söderlundh; 2013). Research across contexts has highlighted the heterogeneity with which EMI policies are implemented across classrooms (Ali, 2013, in Malaysia; Doiz & Lasagabaster, 2017, in Spain; Evans, 2008,

Conclusion 67

in Hong Kong). In a study by Aizawa and Rose (2019), teachers and students at a university in Japan reported that the official language of instruction of their classes was often not followed in practice. Similarly, Ali (2013) found discrepancies between national-level EMI policies and the teaching practices reported by lecturers in Malaysia. This book has added further evidence to these findings on flexible language use in practice through the use of classroom observations at multiple HEIs in Turkey.

Specifically, this book has argued that the variation in EMI implementation occurs *across* and *within* universities in Turkey. Even teachers within the same department differed in their classroom language practices, suggesting that EMI content teachers served as the "final arbiters" of language policy (Johnson, 2013; Johnson & Johnson, 2015).

Johnson and Johnson (2015) define language policy arbiters as "individuals who have a disproportionate amount of impact on language policy and educational programs" (p. 222). Figure 6.1 summarizes the EMI policy arbiters in Turkish higher education, as found in this book. The figure illustrates the dynamics contributing to EMI implementation and notes key arbiters at each level. Although EMI content lecturers had little influence over official EMI policy, they were found to be "the final arbiters" of its classroom implementation. Thus, how teachers' responded to EMI policy contributed to its implementation in practice.

As Figure 6.1 demonstrates, the findings of this study have suggested that the creation of EMI policy occurred largely at the national level, through the formal policy structures of YÖK, which was responsible for approving EMI programs and establishing English proficiency criteria for teachers. Elements of EMI policy were interpreted by institutional actors, including the EMI department heads, who adapted YÖK's decisions in their program curricula. While some aspects of policy appropriation occurred at the institutional or

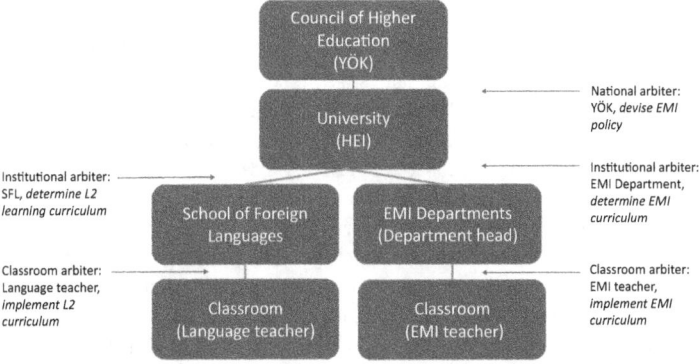

Figure 6.1 EMI language policy arbiters in Turkish higher education

departmental levels (e.g., adding additional criteria for L2 proficiency, devising EMI curricula, etc.), EMI policy implementation was found to be shaped by the classroom practices of individual EMI teachers, who enacted the language practices they perceived as appropriate for their classroom contexts. When policy implementation is considered across macro-, meso-, and micro-levels (Aizawa & Rose, 2019; Ali, 2013), the results of this study have indicated that macro-level policy has not fully "trickled down" to micro-level practices. Issues transferring macro-level policy to micro-level practices could be due to the absence of clear policy implementers at the meso- (institutional and departmental) level: it was not clear *who* did *what* to ensure that EMI policies were implemented at the institutional and department levels, resulting in a lack of (perceived) oversight. Further, as indicated by Figure 6.1, language instructors in the School of Foreign Languages (SFL) were found to be important meso-level actors because they were responsible for administering the English preparatory program (EPP, or *hazırlık*). As such, English language teachers in the SFL were the gatekeepers to EMI study. However, they were removed from classroom teaching and learning in EMI departments (i.e., engineering departments). Despite calls from researchers for increased collaboration between language and content teachers (Dearden et al., 2016; Lasagabaster, 2018; Wilkinson, 2013), this book found evidence of such collaboration only at the Environmental Engineering Department of Large-2. As such, in addition to understanding policy implementation vertically (e.g., macro to micro), this book argues that greater coordination is needed *horizontally* between actors (e.g., EMI departments and SFL; content and language teachers) to ensure the successful implementation of EMI.

6.2 L2 proficiency and linguistic preparedness for EMI

This book adds to the existing research on EMI in Turkey, which suggests a situation of "deep concern in terms of [students'] level of English in general and vocabulary knowledge in particular" (Macaro, Curle, et al., 2018, p. 52). Even though EMI policy in Turkey has established the EPP, the findings of this study have suggested that many students were perceived to lack the English skills necessary for EMI courses. This concurs with the finding of previous research in Turkey, which has highlighted a range of language issues (e.g., Kılıçkaya, 2006; Kırkgöz, 2009, 2014; Sert, 2008).

Participants across universities showcased in this book identified two main areas in which the English language curriculum of the EPP could be revised in order to prepare students more adequately for EMI study: speaking and technical vocabulary (see Macaro, 2019, for the discussion of technical vocabulary). Other studies conducted on EMI in Turkey have produced similar findings (Dalkız, 2002; Sert, 2008; Yıldız et al., 2017). In a study conducted by Soruç and Griffiths (2018) at a university in Istanbul, the difficulties most commonly reported by EMI students were understanding vocabulary used in lectures and

Conclusion 69

inferring vocabulary from context; students also reported difficulty speaking English in class.

Although teachers and students identified speaking as an area of concern in Chapter 5 of this book, the extent to which speaking difficulties impeded students' learning in EMI classes remains unclear. Chapter 4 has shown that Turkish and English were used fluidly in EMI classes, with translanguaging practices facilitating students' communication and participation. As argued in Chapter 2, early research on EMI in Turkey often framed L1 use as the result of insufficient L2 English skills, but recent research on translanguaging has challenged this deficit perspective of L1 use in EMI classes. Instead, translanguaging embraces fluid language use as a natural feature of bilingual communication (Sahan & Rose, 2021). The findings from Chapter 4 add to these recent studies on EMI language use by demonstrating how and why teachers and students make use of their multilingual resources. Nonetheless, teachers and students in interviews (Chapter 5) pointed to language challenges that impeded learning and framed L1 Turkish use as the result of insufficient English skills. These findings suggest a mismatch between the research literature's embrace of translanguaging and practitioners' (teachers' and students') understanding of L1 use as the result of low English proficiency. As Chang (2019) has argued from her research in Taiwan, this mismatch seems to suggest that EMI teachers and students have embraced translanguaging practices but not a translanguaging ideology.

With respect to vocabulary, many students across universities stated that they had not been taught technical vocabulary related to their field in the EPP but learned technical terms by "getting used to" them in EMI lectures (Chapter 5). This finding suggests that students would benefit from targeted and discipline-specific instruction in their English support classes, including during the EPP, to ease the transition to EMI. In their large-scale survey at a university in Hong Kong, Evans and Morrison (2011) found that first-year EMI students experienced difficulty understanding technical vocabulary in their EMI lectures; however, in line with the student comments reported in this book, students' language-related challenges appeared to decrease throughout their studies.

In calling for targeted and discipline-specific English language support classes, this book does not suggest that the EPP should be abolished or that English entry requirements for admission to EMI programs should be imposed. The preparatory year model allows students to enroll in EMI programs regardless of their educational backgrounds or previous language learning experiences, since they will receive intensive English language support before starting their EMI courses. A strength of this model is that it provides an equal opportunity of access to EMI programs, at least theoretically.

However, the findings from this study (Chapter 5) have suggested that interventions might be needed to improve students' English language education in secondary schools, particularly state schools in rural areas. Shohamy

(2013) has argued that language education policy at any one level of the education system should be considered in relation to the policies of the system as a whole: "the teaching of EMI at universities cannot be detached from broader settings where medium of instruction approaches are implemented" (p. 13). In Turkey, the quality and curricula of English language education should be reevaluated in both the EPP and secondary schools in order to prepare students adequately for EMI study. Macaro (2018, p. 13) has stated that there is a "top-down effect of tertiary on secondary" education. The findings from this study have suggested that there is also a bottom-up effect of secondary on tertiary education in terms of students' linguistic preparedness for EMI study in Turkey—albeit a negative one. The linguistic challenges of EMI at the university level in Turkey appear to be exacerbated by aspects of the secondary school system, such as its emphasis on grammar teaching, standardized testing, and the low levels of L2 proficiency with which students leave the secondary school. Given the trends toward the expansion of EMI in Turkish higher education, the secondary school curriculum for English language education should be reevaluated in light of the linguistic demands of EMI study.

6.3 L1 use in EMI

This book adds to a growing body of research which suggests that the L1 is commonly used in EMI classes (Lo & Macaro, 2012; Kırkgöz et al., 2023; Tarnopolsky & Goodman, 2014). The findings from the observation data (Chapter 4) were supported by interviews and focus groups (Chapter 5) in which teachers and students reported L1 Turkish as a useful resource for content learning.

While previous research has suggested that the L1 is used in EMI classrooms primarily to establish rapport and translate technical vocabulary (e.g., Evans, 2008; Söderlundh, 2013; Tarnopolsky & Goodman, 2014), the results presented in Chapter 4 found that the two most common functions of L1 use were "present new content" and "ask questions related to content." In other words, L1 Turkish was used for content teaching and learning. Moreover, instances of vocabulary translation were not found frequently in the data gathered for this book. The student profiles of the EMI classes included in this study may have contributed to this finding, as the sample consisted primarily of home (local, Turkish) students who shared an L1 with their teachers (also Turkish nationals). Moreover, extended explanations in Turkish may have negated the need to translate specific vocabulary items. Indeed, the majority of research on translanguaging in EMI classrooms in Turkey has looked at contexts in which both teachers and students shared an L1 (Ataş, 2023; Inci-Kavak & Kırkgöz, 2022; Kırkgöz et al., 2023). Teachers' and students' language practices might have been different in more linguistically diverse EMI classes—although this study found evidence of EMI teachers employing the L1 when international students were present, contradicting reported practices in Karakas (2016).

Although extended student utterances were limited in the classroom observation data (Chapter 4), student-talk and teacher-student interactions were found to occur most often in Turkish and to incorporate translanguaging practices, respectively. While the findings presented in this book do not go so far as to suggest a relationship between L1 use and teacher-student interaction, other research looking at EMI classroom interaction has found that English-only classrooms were less interactive than L1 learning environments (Lo & Macaro, 2012; Pun & Macaro, 2019). Lo and Macaro (2012) found that EMI resulted in more teacher-centered instruction with "fewer opportunities for negotiation of meaning and scaffolding" (p. 29) compared to L1 MoI classes. The case studies presented in Chapter 4 have demonstrated how some EMI teachers in Turkey scaffolded language and content to encourage participation and learning in English, although the case studies also suggest that EMI teachers would benefit from formal pedagogical training in this area. The majority of teachers (n = 19) included in the study for this book had not received formal pedagogical training of any kind. As such, their translanguaging practice and student-centered pedagogies appeared ad hoc, based on the teachers' perceptions of effective practices rather than evidence-based research. Similar findings were reported by Lasagabaster (2017) in Spain, where L1 use by CLIL secondary school teachers was found to be arbitrary or based on teachers' beliefs and intuition.

Although research on EMI pedagogy is limited, researchers have suggested that student-centered learning might be an effective pedagogical approach in EMI classrooms (Lo & Macaro, 2012; Wilkinson, 2013). As shown in the case studies in Chapter 4, some EMI teachers in Turkey are already striving to scaffold language and content through questioning techniques that increased student participation in English. However, the quality of student output in these lessons was minimal, with responses typically limited to single words or short phrases. These findings support those of Genc and Yuksel (2021) to suggest that EMI teachers in Turkey do not use questioning sequences effectively to encourage extended student outputs in English.

6.4 Dual aims of EMI

Based on the discussion of L2 proficiency and L1 use in EMI classes, this book has found a tension between the stated aims of national-level EMI policy (i.e., English learning *through* EMI) and the mechanisms in place for EMI programs (i.e., English learning *before* EMI). While the definition of EMI used in this book (Macaro, 2018) does not include explicit language learning aims (see Chapter 1), the results of the policy analysis presented in Chapter 3 have found that language learning is a national policy aim in Turkey: "the aim of instruction in a foreign language is to ensure that graduates . . . gain foreign language competences related to their fields" (Article 5, Law No. 29662). However, national and institutional EMI policies were found to support students' L2 English learning *before* EMI classes but not *after* students were *engaged* in EMI learning, though some EMI program curricula included additional EAP courses. Other studies (e.g., Jiang et al., 2019, in China; Moncada-Comas & Block, 2019, in Spain; Unterberger, 2012, in Austria) have noted similar discrepancies between EMI policy aims for language learning and a lack of support for language learning in EMI curricula; however, none of these studies have incorporated data from both policy and classroom observations—a notable contribution of this book.

The findings from this book call into question the theoretical dual aims of content and language learning in EMI (Block & Moncada-Comas, 2019; Rose et al., 2019). While the current study did not objectively measure students' L2 English proficiency, the findings from classroom observations presented in Chapter 4 indicate that EMI content teachers rarely provided focus-on-form instruction. These findings are in line with other studies in the literature, which have suggested that EMI content teachers do not perceive themselves as language teachers nor do they perceive language learning as a primary objective in their courses (Airey, 2012; Ali, 2013; Block & Moncada-Comas, 2019; Dearden & Macaro, 2016; Unterberger, 2012). Moreover, the observed EMI classes were generally teacher-centered lectures with low levels of teacher–student interaction. In some classes, Turkish was the primary language of instruction or the primary language used during teacher-student interactions, making it unlikely that students would have opportunities to develop their communicative English skills without additional, external support.

Still, these findings challenge the notion that EMI is becoming "CLIL-ized" (Moncada-Comas & Block, 2019) in its implementation at Turkish universities. "CLIL-ized EMI" occurs when language learning objectives are incorporated into EMI teaching—in other words, EMI programs begin to resemble CLIL programs (at least theoretically) when language learning becomes an explicit aim. While language learning was found to be a national-level EMI policy objective, EMI classroom practices indicated "no pedagogical moves towards a true CLIL-ization of EMI" (Moncada-Comas & Block, 2019, p. 14), reflecting findings from Spain. Nonetheless, while participants perceived difficulties associated with studying through EMI (Chapter 5), they did not necessarily perceive long-term detrimental effects to content learning. This is in line with Rose et al.'s (2019) findings in Japan that "students from all levels of proficiency were able to pass the course" (p. 10), despite the relationship found between L2 English proficiency and academic success. Thus, in Turkey, EMI classroom practices and policy implementation do not appear to support the supposed dual aims of EMI.

6.5 Summary of the book

By investigating the variation with which EMI is implemented in Turkish HE, this book has called into question what is meant by the role of English in EMI (e.g., Dafouz & Smit, 2016; Macaro, 2019; Kuteeva, 2020). In other words, it has suggested that the "E" in EMI is not monolithic. The EMI engineering courses included in this study were neither English-only nor English-always in their implementation. At the beginning of this book, EMI was defined as: "The use of the English language to teach academic subjects (other than English itself) in countries or jurisdictions where the first language (L1) of the majority of the population is not English" (Macaro, 2018, p. 19). As Macaro (2019) has noted, this definition is "deliberatively provocative" (p. 2), since each aspect of it could be problematized in comparing EMI implementation across contexts and academic disciplines (see Rose et al., 2021). The diversity of classroom language practices observed in this study has not only highlighted the ways in which English is used for teaching and learning in EMI classes, but it has also highlighted the ways in which Turkish and translanguaging practices are used for teaching and learning in EMI. These diverse language practices problematize the scope of what is meant by using English *to teach* academic content in EMI settings.

This book has found the following:

- **With respect to EMI policy**: EMI policies at both the national and institutional levels were primarily concerned with L2 learning through the EPP, which was administered by the SFL as a prerequisite for EMI programs. Policy provisions were found to support L2 learning *before* EMI courses but not *after* students and teachers had met the L2 English proficiency requirements for EMI. As such, there appeared to be a tension between stated policy aims of learning English *through* EMI and the mechanisms in place to support English learning *before* EMI.
- **With respect to classroom language use**: flexible language use, characterized by L1 Turkish and translanguaging practices, occurred frequently in the EMI classes. However, variation was observed across the 21 teachers' EMI classes, with some lessons found to be more teacher-centered and English-dominant than others. The case studies presented in Chapter 4 have illustrated the diversity of language practices with respect to language choice, EMI pedagogical approach, and teacher-student interaction.
- **With respect to perceptions of EMI for teaching and learning**: teachers and students perceived language-related challenges which contributed to the difficulty of learning through English. To overcome language-related challenges, teachers and students perceived the L1 to be a useful resource in EMI classes, thus not only confirming the findings from the classroom observations but also suggesting that EMI teachers and students have yet to embrace a translanguaging ideology.

6.6 Implications for policy, practice, and research

This book has taken a country-wide approach in examining EMI policies, practices, and perceptions in Turkey. Its conclusions offer implications for policymakers, researchers, and practitioners in Turkey and beyond.

Conclusion

A key finding in this book was the perception that students lacked the English proficiency needed for EMI, despite having completed the EPP. University-level education should not be considered in isolation from the broader educational context. In order for students to be linguistically prepared for EMI, educational reforms are needed at the secondary school level to improve English language learning. In particular, the school curriculum should be revised to provide more emphasis on communicative skills such as speaking and listening (Kamaşak et al., 2021). As the number of EMI programs—and thus the number of EMI students—continues to grow in Turkey, it is imperative that students are provided with adequate English language instructions prior to entering university. Strengthening the quality of English instruction in secondary schools would provide students with a better foundation before entering the EPP, which could then focus on students' discipline-specific academic English needs.

Even with the EPP, EMI students in Turkey continue to struggle with the linguistic demands of EMI. As such, ongoing language support after the preparatory year is needed to build students' confidence and ability to participate in EMI courses. Examples of continuous language support could include collaboration between content and language instructors to address students' needs, such as the example found at Large-2 in this book.

This book also offers theoretical implications for EMI researchers. Theoretical understandings of EMI must recognize the diversity of language practices that characterize EMI university classes. In other words, the scope of the "E" in EMI should be expanded to see English as *a* language of instruction but not *the only* language of instruction (Graham et al., 2021). More clarity of definition is needed to evaluate and compare EMI research contexts (Rose et al., 2021). While this book has argued that L1 use is a commonplace feature of EMI, it has challenged notions of EMI becoming "CLIL-ized" (Moncada-Comas & Block, 2019), at least in the Turkish context. This book has shown that EMI content teachers rarely focus on form or aspects of language in their lectures, and it has argued that policy does not make any provision for the integration of content and language learning. Given these findings, stakeholders and researchers should reevaluate the assumption that EMI is effective for language learning. If language learning is an aim of EMI policy—as found in Chapter 3—language learning objectives should be included in EMI curricula and supported by pedagogical practices that optimize conditions for language development. Such revisions to EMI curricula and pedagogy would improve the alignment of policy and practice, and appropriate pedagogical training for EMI lecturers would help to achieve these goals.

The scope of this book has been limited to undergraduate EMI programs in engineering departments in Turkey. Different results might be found in other academic disciplines, such as in the social sciences or humanities, and future research is encouraged in this area. Similarly, further research is needed into language use and teacher-student interactions in EMI settings to provide a richer understanding of student-talk in EMI classrooms. Looking at student output will help us understand whether and how EMI might contribute to the development of students' communicative English skills.

With respect to the quality and equality of education, it is important that teachers and students across institutional contexts are provided with adequate preparation and ongoing support to enable optimal conditions for EMI success. Researchers, policymakers, and practitioners should carefully consider the purposes and intended learning outcomes of EMI programs, and they should ensure that teachers and students are supported to meet these aims.

References

Airey, J. (2012). 'I don't teach language': The linguistic attitudes of physics lecturers in Sweden. *AILA Review*, *25*, 64–79. https://doi.org/10.1075/aila.25.05air

Aizawa, I., & Rose, H. (2019). An analysis of Japan's English as medium of instruction initiatives within higher education: The gap between meso-level policy and micro-level practice. *Higher Education*, *77*(6), 1125–1142. https://doi.org/10.1007/s10734-018-0323-5

Ali, N. L. (2013). A changing paradigm in language planning: English-medium instruction policy at the tertiary level in Malaysia. *Current Issues in Language Planning*, *14*(1), 73–92. https://doi.org/10.1080/14664208.2013.775543

Alptekin, C., & Tatar, S. (2011). Research on foreign language teaching and learning in Turkey (2005–2009). *Language Teaching*, *44*(3), 328–353. https://doi.org/10.1017/S026144481100005X

Altay, M., Curle, S., Yuksel, D., & Soruç, A. (2022). Investigating academic achievement of English medium instruction courses in Turkey. *Studies in Second Language Learning and Teaching*, *12*(1), 117–141. https://doi.org/10.14746/ssllt.2022.12.1.6

Altay, M., & Yüksel, D. (2021). Job prospects of different EMI engineering programmes' graduates. *Participatory Educational Research*, *8*(2), 460–475. https://doi.org/10.17275/per.21.49.8.2

An, J., Macaro, E., & Childs, A. (2021). Classroom interaction in EMI high schools: Do teachers who are native speakers of English make a difference? *System*, *98*, 102482. https://doi.org/10.1016/j.system.2021.102482

Annamalai, E. (2013). India's economic restructuring with English: Benefits versus costs. In J. W. Tollefson (Ed.), *Language policies in education: Critical issues* (2nd ed) (pp. 191–207). Routledge.

Aslan, M. (2018). The debate on English-medium instruction and globalisation in the Turkish context: A sociopolitical perspective. *Journal of Multilingual and Multicultural Development*, *39*(7), 602–616. https://doi.org/10.1080/01434632.2017.1417413

Ataş, U. (2023). Translanguaging in English-Medium Instruction (EMI): Examining English literature content classrooms. *Turkish Journal of Education*, *12*(3), 142–157. https://doi.org/10.19128/turje.1210174

Baker, W., & Hüttner, J. (2017). English and more: A multisite study of roles and conceptualisations of language in English medium multilingual universities from Europe to Asia. *Journal of Multilingual and Multicultural Development*, *38*(6), 501–516. https://doi.org/10.1080/01434632.2016.1207183

Başıbek, N., Dolmacı, M., Cengiz, B. C., Bür, B., Dilek, Y., & Kara, B. (2014). Lecturers' perceptions of English medium instruction at engineering departments of higher education: A study on partial English medium instruction at some state universities in Turkey. *Procedia—Social and Behavioral Sciences, 116*, 1819–1825. https://doi.org/10.1016/j.sbspro.2014.01.477

Block, D., & Moncada-Comas, B. (2019). English-medium instruction in higher education and the ELT gaze: STEM lecturers' self-positioning as NOT English language teachers. *International Journal of Bilingual Education and Bilingualism, 25*(2), 401–417. https://doi.org/10.1080/13670050.2019.1689917

Bozbiyik, M., & Morton, T. (2023). Transitioning between "outside" and "inside" knowledge in an online university EMI chemistry course. *Applied Linguistics, 44*(2), 265–286. https://doi.org/10.1093/applin/amac068

Bozdoğan, D., & Karlıdağ, B. (2013). A case of CLIL practice in the Turkish context: Lending an ear to students. *Asian EFL Journal*.

Bradford, A., & Brown, H. (2017). ROAD-MAPPING English-medium instruction in Japan. In A. Bradford & H. Brown (Eds.), *English-medium instruction in Japanese higher education: Policy, challenges and outcomes*. Multilingual Matters.

Brenn-White, M., & Faethe, E. (2013). *English-taught masters programs in Europe: A 2013 update*. Institute of International Education, Center for Academic Mobility Research.

Büyükkantarcıoğlu, N. (2004). A sociolinguistic analysis of the present dimensions of English as a foreign language in Turkey. *International Journal of the Sociology of Language, 2004*(165), 33–58. https://doi.org/10.1515/ijsl.2004.006

Chang, S. Y. (2019). Beyond the English box: Constructing and communicating knowledge through translingual practices in the higher education classroom. *English Teaching & Learning, 43*(1), 23–40. https://doi.org/10.1007/s42321-018-0014-4

Coleman, J. A. (2006). English-medium teaching in European higher education. *Language Teaching, 39*(1), 1–14. https://doi.org/10.1017/S026144480600320X

Costa, F., & Coleman, J. A. (2012). A survey of English-medium instruction in Italian higher education. *International Journal of Bilingual Education and Bilingualism, 16*(1), 3–19. https://doi.org/10.1080/13670050.2012.676621

Coyle, D., Hood, P., & Marsh, D. (2010). *Content and language integrated learning*. Cambridge University Press.

Creese, A., & Blackledge, A. (2015). Translanguaging and identity in educational settings. *Annual Review of Applied Linguistics, 35*, 20–35. https://doi.org/10.1017/S0267190514000233

Curle, S., Yuksel, D., Soruç, A., & Altay, M. (2020). Predictors of English medium instruction academic success: English proficiency versus first language medium. *System, 95*. https://doi.org/10.1016/j.system.2020.102378

Dafouz, E. (2018). English-medium instruction and teacher education programmes in higher education: Ideological forces and imagined identities at work. *International Journal of Bilingual Education and Bilingualism, 21*(5), 540–552. https://doi.org/10.1080/13670050.2018.1487926

Dafouz, E., Hüttner, J., & Smit, U. (2016). University teachers' beliefs of language and content integration in English-medium education in multilingual university settings. In T. Nikula, E. Dafouz, P. Moore, & U. Smit (Eds.), *Conceptualising integration in CLIL and multilingual education* (pp. 123–144). Multilingual Matters.

Dafouz, E., & Smit, U. (2016). Towards a dynamic conceptual framework for English-medium Education in multilingual university settings. *Applied Linguistics, 37*(3), 397–415. https://doi.org/10.1093/applin/amu034

References

Dafouz, E., & Smit, U. (2020). *ROAD-MAPPING English medium education in the internationalised university*. Palgrave Macmillan.

Dalkız, A. (2002). *Ortaöğretimde İngilizce kimya eğitiminin başarıya etkisi [The impact of middle school chemistry education in English on academic success]*. Unpublished Masters' dissertation. Marmara University.

De Costa, P. I., Park, J., & Wee, L. (2019). Linguistic entrepreneurship as affective regime: Organizations, audit culture, and second/foreign language education policy. *Language Policy, 18*(3), 387–406. https://doi.org/10.1007/s10993-018-9492-4

Dearden, J., & Akincioglu, M. (2016). *EMI in Turkish universities: Collaborative planning and student voices*. Oxford University Press.

Dearden, J., & Macaro, E. (2016). Higher education teachers' attitudes towards English medium instruction: A three-country comparison. *Studies in Second Language Learning and Teaching, 6*(3), 455–486. https://doi.org/10.14746/sllt.2016.6.3.5

Dearden, J., Macaro, E., & Akincioglu, M. (2016). English medium instruction in universities: A collaborative experiment in Turkey. *Studies in English Language Teaching, 4*(1), 51–76. https://doi.org/10.22158/selt.v4n1p51

Doiz, A., & Lasagabaster, D. (2017). Management teams and teaching staff: Do they share the same beliefs about obligatory CLIL programmes and the use of the L1? *Language and Education, 31*(2), 93–109. https://doi.org/10.1080/09500782.2017.1290102

Doiz, A., Lasagabaster, D., & Sierra, J. M. (2013). English as L3 at a bilingual university in the Basque Country. In A. Doiz, D. Lasagabaster, & J. M. Sierra (Eds.), *English-medium instruction at universities: Global challenges* (pp. 84–105). Multilingual Matters.

Duran, D., Kurhila, S., & Sert, O. (2022). Word search sequences in teacher–student interaction in an English as medium of instruction context. *International Journal of Bilingual Education and Bilingualism, 25*(2), 502–521. https://doi.org/10.1080/13670050.2019.1703896

Duran, D., & Sert, O. (2019). Preference organization in English as a medium of instruction classrooms in a Turkish higher education setting. *Linguistics and Education, 49*, 72–85. https://doi.org/10.1016/j.linged.2018.12.006

Ege, F., Yuksel, D., & Curle, S. (2022). A corpus-based analysis of discourse strategy use by English-medium instruction university lecturers in Turkey. *Journal of English for Academic Purposes, 58*, 101125. https://doi.org/10.1016/j.jeap.2022.101125

Ekoç, A. (2020). English medium instruction (EMI) from the perspectives of students at a technical university in Turkey. *Journal of Further and Higher Education, 44*(2), 231–243. https://doi.org/10.1080/0309877X.2018.1527025

Evans, S. (2008). Classroom language use in Hong Kong's reformed English-medium stream. *Journal of Multilingual and Multicultural Development, 29*(6), 483–498. https://doi.org/10.1080/01434630802147940

Evans, S., & Morrison, B. (2011). Meeting the challenges of English-medium higher education: The first-year experience in Hong Kong. *English for Specific Purposes, 30*(3), 198–208. https://doi.org/10.1016/j.esp.2011.01.001

Ferguson, G. (2009). What next? Towards an agenda for classroom codeswitching research. *International Journal of Bilingual Education and Bilingualism, 12*(2), 231–241. https://doi.org/10.1080/13670050802153236

Galloway, N., & Rose, H. (2021). English medium instruction and the English language practitioner. *ELT Journal, 75*(1), 33–41. https://doi.org/10.1093/elt/ccaa063

References

García, O., & Wei, L. (2014). *Translanguaging: Language, bilingualism and education*. Palgrave Macmillan.

Genc, E., & Yuksel, D. (2021). Teacher questions in English medium instruction classrooms in a Turkish higher education setting. *Linguistics and Education, 66,* 100992. https://doi.org/10.1016/j.linged.2021.100992

Graham, K. M., Eslami, Z. R., & Hillman, S. (2021). From English as the medium to English as a medium: Perspectives of EMI students in Qatar. *System, 99,* 102508. https://doi.org/10.1016/j.system.2021.102508

Günay, D., & Günay, A. (2011). 1933'den Günümüze Türk Yükseköğretiminde Niceliksel Gelişmeler [Quantitative developments in Turkish higher education since 1933]. *Yükseköğretim ve Bilim Dergisi, 1*(1), 1–22.

Hopkyns, S., & Gkonou, C. (2023). Sites of belonging: Fluctuating and entangled emotions at a UAE English-medium university. *Linguistics and Education, 75,* 101148. https://doi.org/10.1016/j.linged.2023.101148

Hu, G., & Lei, J. (2014). English-medium instruction in Chinese higher education: A case study. *Higher Education, 67*(5), 551–567. https://doi.org/10.1007/s10734-013-9661-5

Hultgren, A. K. (2013). Lexical borrowing from English into Danish in the sciences: An empirical investigation of "domain loss". *International Journal of Applied Linguistics, 23*(2), 166–182. https://doi.org/10.1111/j.1473-4192.2012.00324.x

Inci-Kavak, V. İ., & Kirkgöz, Y. (2022). Exploring university students' note-taking in literature courses: A translanguaging perspective. *Cukurova University Faculty of Education Journal, 51*(2), 1468–1486.

Jiang, L., Zhang, L. J., & May, S. (2019). Implementing English medium instruction (EMI) in China: Teachers' practices and perceptions, and students' learning motivation and needs. *International Journal of Bilingual Education and Bilingualism, 22*(2), 107–119. https://doi.org/10.1080/13670050.2016.1231166

Johnson, D. C. (2013). Positioning the language policy arbiter: Governmentality and footing in the school district of Philadelphia. Critical issues in language policy in education. In J. W. Tollefson (Ed.), *Language policies in education: Critical issues* (2nd ed) (pp. 116–136). Routledge.

Johnson, D. C., & Johnson, E. J. (2015). Power and agency in language policy appropriation. *Language Policy, 14*(3), 221–243. https://doi.org/10.1007/s10993-014-9333-z

Kamaşak, R., & Sahan, K. (2023). Academic Success in English medium courses: Exploring student challenges, opinions, language proficiency and L2 use. *RELC Journal*. https://doi.org/10.1177/00336882231167611

Kamaşak, R., Sahan, K., & Rose, H. (2021). Academic language-related challenges at an English-medium university. *Journal of English for Academic Purposes, 49,* 100945. https://doi.org/10.1016/j.jeap.2020.100945

Karakas, A. (2016). Turkish lecturers' views on the place of mother tongue in the teaching of content courses through English medium. *Asian Englishes, 18*(3), 242–257. https://doi.org/10.1080/13488678.2016.1229831

Karakaş, A. (2023). Translanguaging in content-based EMI classes through the lens of Turkish students: Self-reported practices, functions and orientations. *Linguistics and Education, 77,* 101221. https://doi.org/10.1016/j.linged.2023.101221

Kemaloglu-Er, E. (2023). Feeling in-between experienced by tertiary-level English preparatory students: An investigation of two Turkish EMI universities. *Learn. Journal, 16*(2), 366–378.

Kerklaan, V., Moreira, G., & Boersma, K. (2008). The Role of Language in the Internationalisation of Higher Education: An example from Portugal. *European Journal of Education, 43*(2), 241–255. https://doi.org/10.1111/j.1465-3435.2008.00349.x

Kılıçkaya, F. (2006). Instructors' attitudes towards English-medium instruction in Turkey. *Humanising Language Teaching Journal, 8*(6), 1–16.

Kırkgöz, Y. (2007). Language planning and implementation in Turkish primary schools. *Current Issues in Language Planning, 8*(2), 174–191. https://doi.org/10.2167/cilp114.0

Kırkgöz, Y. (2009). Students' and lecturers' perceptions of the effectiveness of foreign language instruction in an English-medium university in Turkey. *Teaching in Higher Education, 14*(1), 81–93. https://doi.org/10.1080/13562510802602640

Kırkgöz, Y. (2014). Students' perceptions of English language versus Turkish language used as the medium of instruction in higher education in Turkey. *Turkish Studies, 9*(12), 443–459.

Kırkgöz, Y., İnci-Kavak, V., Karakaş, A., & Panero, S. M. (2023). Translanguaging practices in Turkish EMI classrooms: Commonalities and differences across two academic disciplines. *System, 113*, 102982. https://doi.org/10.1016/j.system.2023.102982

Kırkgöz, Y., & Küçük, C. (2021). Investigating translanguaging practices in an English medium higher education context in Turkey: A case of two lecturers. In B. Di Sabato & B. Hughes (Eds.), *Multilingual perspectives from Europe and beyond on language policy and practice* (pp. 135–155). Routledge.

Kirkpatrick, A. (2011). Internationalization or Englishization: Medium of instruction in today's universities. *Hong Kong: Center for governance and citizenship*. The Hong Kong Institute of Education.

Kuteeva, M. (2019). Researching English-medium instruction at Swedish universities: Developments over the past decade. In K. Murata (Ed.), *English-medium instruction from an English as a lingua franca perspective* (pp. 46–63). Routledge.

Kuteeva, M. (2020). Revisiting the "E" in EMI: Students' perceptions of standard English, lingua franca and translingual practices. *International Journal of Bilingual Education and Bilingualism, 23*(3), 287–300. https://doi.org/10.1080/13670050.2019.1637395

Lasagabaster, D. (2017). 'I always speak English in my classes': Reflections on the use of the L1/L2 in English-medium instruction." In A. Llinares & T. Morton (Eds.), *Applied linguistics perspectives on CLIL* (pp. 259–275). John Benjamins Publishing Company.

Lasagabaster, D. (2018). Fostering team teaching: Mapping out a research agenda for English-medium instruction at university level. *Language Teaching, 51*(3), 400–416. https://doi.org/10.1017/S0261444818000113

Lasagabaster, D., & Sierra, J. M. (2010). Immersion and CLIL in English: More differences than similarities. *ELT Journal, 64*(4), 367–375. https://doi.org/10.1093/elt/ccp082

Lin, A. (2012). Multilingual and multimodal resources in genre-based pedagogical approaches to L2 English content classrooms. In C. Leung & B. V. Street (Eds.), *English: A changing medium for education* (pp. 79–103). Multilingual Matters.

Lo, Y. Y., & Macaro, E. (2012). The medium of instruction and classroom interaction: Evidence from Hong Kong secondary schools. *International Journal of Bilingual Education and Bilingualism, 15*(1), 29–52. https://doi.org/10.1080/13670050.2011.588307

References

Macaro, E. (2018). *English medium instruction: Content and language in policy and practice.* Oxford University Press.

Macaro, E. (2019). Exploring the role of language in English medium instruction. *International Journal of Bilingual Education and Bilingualism, 23*(3), 263–276. https://doi.org/10.1080/13670050.2019.1620678

Macaro, E., & Akincioglu, M. (2018). Turkish university students' perceptions about English medium instruction: Exploring year group, gender and university type as variables. *Journal of Multilingual and Multicultural Development, 39*(3), 256–270. https://doi.org/10.1080/01434632.2017.1367398

Macaro, E., Curle, S., Pun, J., An, J., & Dearden, J. (2018). A systematic review of English medium instruction in higher education. *Language Teaching, 51*(1), 36–76. https://doi.org/10.1017/S0261444817000350

Macaro, E., Tian, L., & Chu, L. (2018). First and second language use in English medium instruction contexts. *Language Teaching Research, 24*(3), 382–402. https://doi.org/10.1177/1362168818783231

Menken, K. (2008). *English learners left behind: Standardized testing as language policy.* Clevedon, UK: Multilingual Matters.

Moncada-Comas, B., & Block, D. (2019). CLIL-ised EMI in practice: Issues arising. *Language Learning Journal, 49*(6), 686–698. https://doi.org/10.1080/09571736.2019.1660704

Morton, T. (2012). Classroom talk, conceptual change and teacher reflection in bilingual science teaching. *Teaching and Teacher Education, 28*(1), 101–110.

Paulsrud, B., Tian, Z., & Toth, J. (Eds.). (2021). *English-medium instruction and translanguaging* (Vol. 126). Multilingual Matters.

Pecorari, D., & Malmström, H. (2018). At the crossroads of TESOL and English medium instruction. *TESOL Quarterly, 52*(3), 497–515. https://doi.org/10.1002/tesq.470

Phillipson, R. (2008). Lingua franca or lingua frankensteinia? English in European integration and globalisation. *World Englishes, 27*(2), 250–267. https://doi.org/10.1111/j.1467-971X.2008.00555.x

Piller, I., & Cho, J. (2013). Neoliberalism as language policy. *Language in Society, 42*(1), 23–44. https://doi.org/10.1017/S0047404512000887

Pun, J., & Macaro, E. (2019). The effect of first and second language use on question types in English medium instruction science classrooms in Hong Kong. *International Journal of Bilingual Education and Bilingualism, 22*(1), 64–77. https://doi.org/10.1080/13670050.2018.1510368

Rose, H., Curle, S., Aizawa, I., & Thompson, G. (2019). What drives success in English medium taught courses? The interplay between language proficiency, academic skills, and motivation. *Studies in Higher Education, 45*(11), 2149–2161. https://doi.org/10.1080/03075079.2019.1590690

Rose, H., Macaro, E., Sahan, K., Aizawa, I., Zhou, S., & Wei, M. (2021). Defining English medium instruction: Striving for comparative equivalence. *Language Teaching*, 1–12.

Rose, H., & McKinley, J. (2018). Japan's English medium instruction initiatives and the globalization of higher education. *Higher Education, 75*(1), 111–129. https://doi.org/10.1007/s10734-017-0125-1

Rose, H., Sahan, K., & Zhou, S. (2022). Global English medium instruction: Perspectives at the crossroads of Global Englishes and EMI. *Asian Englishes, 24*(2), 160–172. https://doi.org/10.1080/13488678.2022.2056794

Sah, P. K. (2022). English medium instruction in South Asia's multilingual schools: Unpacking the dynamics of ideological orientations, policy/practices, and democratic questions. *International Journal of Bilingual Education and Bilingualism*, *25*(2), 742–755. https://doi.org/10.1080/13670050.2020.1718591

Sah, P. K., & Li, G. (2018). English medium instruction (EMI) as linguistic capital in Nepal: Promises and realities. *International Multilingual Research Journal*, *12*(2), 109–123. https://doi.org/10.1080/19313152.2017.1401448

Sahan, K. (2020). *Variations of English-medium instruction: Comparing policy and practice in Turkish higher education* [Unpublished doctoral dissertation]. University of Oxford.

Sahan, K. (2022). Provision for partial English-medium instruction programmes in Turkish higher education: All or nothing? In J. McKinley & N. Galloway (Eds.), *English-medium instruction practices in higher education, International perspectives* (pp. 85–97). Bloomsbury Publishing.

Sahan, K., Galloway, N., & McKinley, J. (2022). 'English-only' English medium instruction: Mixed views in Thai and Vietnamese higher education. *Language Teaching Research*. https://doi.org/10.1177/13621688211072632

Sahan, K., Kamaşak, R., & Rose, H. (2023). The interplay of motivated behaviour, self-concept, self-efficacy, and language use on ease of academic study in English medium education. *System*, *114*, 103016. https://doi.org/10.1016/j.system.2023.103016

Sahan, K., Mikolajewska, A., Rose, H., Macaro, E., Searle, M., Aizawa, I., Zhou, S., & Veitch, A. (2021). *Global mapping of English as a medium of instruction in higher education: 2020 and beyond*. British Council.

Sahan, K., & Rose, H. (2021). Translanguaging or code-switching? Re-examining the functions of language in EMI classrooms. In B. Di Sabato & B. Hughes (Eds.), *Multilingual perspectives from Europe and beyond on language policy and practice* (pp. 45–62). Routledge.

Sahan, K., & Şahan, Ö. (2021). Investigating student and alumni perspectives on language learning and career prospects through English medium instruction. *Teaching in Higher Education*, 1–22. https://doi.org/10.1080/13562517.2021.1973407

Şahan, Ö., & Sahan, K. (2023). A narrative inquiry into the emotional effects of English medium instruction, language learning, and career opportunities. *Linguistics and Education*, *75*, 101149. https://doi.org/10.1016/j.linged.2023.101149

Sánchez-Pérez, M. D. M. (Ed.). (2020). *Teacher training for English-medium instruction in higher education*. IGI Global.

Selvi, A. F. (2011). World Englishes in the Turkish sociolinguistic context. *World Englishes*, *30*(2), 182–199. https://doi.org/10.1111/j.1467-971X.2011.01705.x

Selvi, A. F. (2014). The medium-of-instruction debate in Turkey: Oscillating between national ideas and bilingual ideals. *Current Issues in Language Planning*, *15*(2), 133–152. https://doi.org/10.1080/14664208.2014.898357

Selvi, A. F. (2020). Qualitative content analysis. In J. McKinley & H. Rose (Eds.), *The Routledge handbook of research methods in applied linguistics* (pp. 440–452). Routledge.

Selvi, A. F. (2022). Resisting English medium instruction through digital grassroots activism. *Journal of Multilingual and Multicultural Development*, *43*(2), 81–97. https://doi.org/10.1080/01434632.2020.1724120

Sert, N. (2008). The language of instruction dilemma in the Turkish context. *System*, *36*(2), 156–171. https://doi.org/10.1016/j.system.2007.11.006

References

Shao, L. (2019). *Case studies of English-medium instruction in higher education: Business programmes in China, Japan and the Netherlands* [Doctoral Dissertation]. University of Dublin, Trinity College Dublin.

Shohamy, E. (2006). *Language policy: Hidden agendas and new approaches*. Routledge.

Shohamy, E. (2013). A critical perspective on the use of English as a medium of instruction at universities. In A. Doiz, D. Lasagabaster, & J. M. Sierra (Eds.), *English-medium instruction at universities: Global challenges* (pp. 196–210). Multilingual Matters.

Sinanoğlu, O. (2004). *Bye bye Türkçe*. Otopsi.

Smit, U., & Dafouz, E. (2012). Integrating content and language in higher education: An introduction to English-medium policies, conceptual issues and research practices across Europe. *AILA Review, 25*, 1–12. https://doi.org/10.1075/aila.25.01smi

Söderlundh, H. (2013). Applying transnational strategies locally: English as a medium of instruction in Swedish higher education. *Nordic Journal of English Studies, 13*(1), 113–132. https://doi.org/10.35360/njes.278

Soruc, A., Altay, M., Curle, S., & Yuksel, D. (2021). Students' academic language-related challenges in English medium instruction: The role of English proficiency and language gain. *System, 103*, 102651. https://doi.org/10.1016/j.system.2021.102651

Soruç, A., Dinler, A., & Griffiths, C. (2018). Listening comprehension strategies of EMI students in Turkey. In Y. Kirkgoz & K. Dikilitas (Eds.), *Key issues in English for specific purposes in higher education* (pp. 265–287). Springer. https://doi.org/10.1007/978-3-319-70214-8_15

Soruç, A., & Griffiths, C. (2018). English as a medium of instruction: Students' strategies. *ELT Journal, 72*(1), 38–48. https://doi.org/10.1093/elt/ccx017

Spolsky, B. (2004). *Language policy*. Cambridge University Press.

Tai, K. W. H., & Wei, L. (2021). Constructing playful talk through translanguaging in English medium instruction mathematics classrooms. *Applied Linguistics, 42*(4), 607–640. https://doi.org/10.1093/applin/amaa043

Tarnopolsky, O. B., & Goodman, B. A. (2014). The ecology of language in classrooms at a university in eastern Ukraine. *Language and Education, 28*(4), 383–396. https://doi.org/10.1080/09500782.2014.890215

Tsui, A. B. M. (1985). Analysing input and interaction in second language classrooms. *RELC Journal, 16*(1), 8–30. https://doi.org/10.1177/003368828501600102

Turhan, B., & Kırkgöz, Y. (2018). Motivation of engineering students and lecturers toward English medium instruction at tertiary level in Turkey. *Journal of Language and Linguistic Studies, 14*(1), 261–277.

Uçar, H. F., & Soruç, A. (2018). Examining Turkish university students' sense of achievement, motivation, and anxiety: A comparison of the English- and French-medium education systems. *Eurasian Journal of Applied Linguistics, 4*(2), 177–191. https://doi.org/10.32601/ejal.464096

Unterberger, B. (2012). English-medium programmes at Austrian business faculties: A status quo survey on national trends and a case study on programme design and delivery. *AILA Review, 25*, 80–100. https://doi.org/10.1075/aila.25.06unt

Wächter, B., & Maiworm, F. (2015). *English-taught programmes in European higher education: The state of play in 2014*. Lemmens.

Wilkinson, R. (2013). English-medium instruction at a Dutch university: Challenges and pitfalls. In A. Doiz, D. Lasagabaster, & J. M. Sierra (Eds.), *English-medium instruction at universities: Global challenges* (pp. 3–24). Multilingual Matters.

References

Yıldız, M., Soruç, A., & Griffiths, C. (2017). Challenges and needs of students in the EMI (English as a medium of instruction) classroom. *Konin Language Studies*, *5*(4), 387–402.

YÖK. (2019). *Yükseköğretim Bilgi Yönetim Sistemi* [*Higher Education Information Management System*]. https://istatistik.yok.gov.tr/

Yuksel, D., Curle, S., & Kaya, S. (2021). What role do language learning mindsets play in English medium instruction? A comparison of engineering and business administration in Turkey. *Journal for the Psychology of Language Learning*, *3*(1), 50–62. https://doi.org/10.52598/jpll/3/1/3

Yuksel, D., Soruç, A., Altay, M., & Curle, S. (2023a). A longitudinal study at an English medium instruction university in Turkey: The interplay between English language improvement and academic success. *Applied Linguistics Review*, *14*(3), 533–552. https://doi.org/10.1515/applirev-2020-0097

Yuksel, D., Soruç, A., Horzum, B., & McKinley, J. (2023b). Examining the role of English language proficiency, language learning anxiety, and self-regulation skills in EMI students' academic success. *Studies in Second Language Learning and Teaching*, *13*(2), 399–426. https://doi.org/10.14746/ssllt.38280

Yuksel, D., Wingrove, P., Zuaro, B., Nao, M., & Hultgren, A. K. (2023c, April 13–14). "Let me say this first . . ." Reactions of stakeholders towards EMI in Turkey. In *ELI-NET first, annual conference*. University of Glasgow.

Zok, D. (2010). Turkey's language revolution and the status of English today. *The English Languages: History, Diaspora, Culture*, *1*(1), 1–14.

Index

academic discipline 14, 20, 22, 25–26, 28, 73, 74
academic lingua franca 10; *see also* English as a lingua franca
agency 27–28, 30, 33, 34; *see also* agents
agents 20, 22, 27–28; *see also* agency
Anadolu liseleri *see* Anatolian high schools
Anatolian high schools 9

beliefs 4, 6, 10, 12, 15, 18, 20, 51, 71; self-beliefs 12; *see also* perceptions
Bilkent University 9
Boğaziçi University 9
Bologna Process 4, 8

career advancement 10
China 1, 4, 72
classroom interaction 15, 34, 49, 71; *see also* teacher-student interaction
classroom observations 1, 6, 7, 13, 14, 15, 17, 34–35, 41, 49, 52, 67, 71–73
classroom practices 5, 8, 11, 14–16, 19, 22, 29, 34–35, 42, 49, 53, 54, 60, 68, 72
codeswitching 34; inter-sentential 40, 41; intra-sentential 40, 41; L1 Turkish use 16, 55, 63, 66, 69

Common European Framework of Reference (CEFR) 14, 24, 33
content and language integrated learning (CLIL) 2–3, 71; CLIL-ized EMI 3, 72, 74
content-based instruction (CBI) 2–3
content learning 2, 13–15, 25, 49, 65, 70, 72
Conversation Analysis 15
Council of Higher Education *see* Yükseköğretim Kurulu (YÖK)

dual aims 1, 42, 66, 71–72

engagement 49
English as a foreign language (EFL) 2–3, 9, 14, 22; *see also* English language teaching (ELT)
English as a lingua franca (ELF) 4; *see also* academic lingua franca
English language teaching (ELT) 2–3, 22, 57–58; *see also* English as a foreign language (EFL)
English-medium instruction (EMI): definition of 2–3, 71, 73–74; challenges 11–16, 44, 47, 49, 51, 59–63, 65, 69–70, 73; growth of 3–4, 8–10; motivations for 3, 5; opposition to 5, 10; partial EMI 19–20, 22, 24–26, 29–30, 33, 53, 55
English preparatory program (EPP) 11–12, 16, 22–25, 28, 56, 58–60, 68–70, 73–74

English proficiency 3, 10, 11–14, 16, 22–25, 26, 27–28, 31, 32–33, 42–43, 47, 55–57, 59, 63–65, 68–70, 72

focus groups 7, 45, 52, 54, 56, 58, 59, 61, 63, 64, 70

Galatasaray Lisesi 9
global market 1; *see also* job market
Hazırlık *see* English preparatory program (EPP)
Higher Education Law 19, 28
Hong Kong 4, 11, 16, 66–67, 69

identity 10, 18; EMI teacher identity 51
immersion 2–3
internationalization 5–6, 20, 22, 30–32, 33
international students 4, 5, 12, 15, 28, 31, 52, 54, 55, 64–65, 69
Italy 1

Japan 1, 4, 19, 20, 67, 72
job market 5, 32

language functions 34, 35, 38–42, 70
language learning 2–3, 11, 13–14, 22, 25, 26, 32–33, 52, 58, 65, 69, 71–74
language management 18, 20, 22, 26–27
language policy 6, 18–20, 26–27, 54–55, 67; language policy and planning 18
language proficiency *see* English proficiency
language support 6, 12, 25, 26, 32–33, 74; discipline-specific language support 69; *see also* English preparatory program (EPP)
learning outcomes 8, 13–14, 50, 75

Malaysia 1, 19, 66–67
Middle East Technical University 9

Milli Eğitim Bakanlığı (MEB) 57–58
motivation 10, 11–12, 45, 62

National Ministry of Education *see* Milli Eğitim Bakanlığı (MEB)
negotiation of meaning 71

pedagogy 49, 71, 74
perceptions 6, 7, 10, 13, 15, 18, 20, 51–53, 57, 59–65, 73–74
policy arbiters 19, 67

ROAD-MAPPING framework 7, 20–22, 25–30
Robert College 8, 9

scaffolding 42, 46, 49, 71
School of Foreign Languages (SFL) 21, 23–25, 26, 27, 32, 67–68, 73
secondary school 9, 11, 23, 57–59, 65, 66, 69–70, 71, 74
semi-structured interviews 7, 42, 52, 69, 70
sociolinguistics 20
Spain 1, 66, 71–72
Spolsky's framework 18
student participation 35, 42, 44, 46, 49, 50, 60–63, 69, 71

teacher-student interaction 16, 37–38, 41–42, 49–50, 71–72, 74
translanguaging 8, 16, 34–35, 41–42, 46, 69, 70–71; translanguaging ideology 63, 65, 69, 73; translanguaging practices 16, 36–38, 46, 49–50, 63, 69, 73

United Arab Emirates 1
Üsküdar American College 9

Yabancı Dil Sınavı (YDS) 10, 23–24, 56–57
Yükseköğretim Kurulu (YÖK) 19, 21, 23, 26–28, 31, 55, 67

For Product Safety Concerns and Information please contact our EU
representative GPSR@taylorandfrancis.com
Taylor & Francis Verlag GmbH, Kaufingerstraße 24, 80331 München, Germany

www.ingramcontent.com/pod-product-compliance
Lightning Source LLC
Chambersburg PA
CBHW051759230426

43670CB00012B/2353